Frogs and Toads

2nd Edition

Steve Grenard

Wiley Publishing, Inc.

Library of Congress Cataloging-in-Publication Data:
Grenard, Steve.
  Frogs and toads / Steve Grenard. — 2nd ed.
    p. cm. — (Your happy healthy pet)
  ISBN 978-0-470-16510-2 (cloth : alk. paper)
1. Frogs as pets. 2. Toads as pets. 3. Frogs. 4. Toads. I. Title.
  SF459.F83G74 2007
  639.3'789—dc22
                            2007018915
Printed in the United States of America

10 9 8 7 6 5 4 3 2 1

2nd Edition

Illustration on page 112 by Brooke Graczyk
Book design by Melissa Auciello-Brogan
Cover design by Michael J. Freeland
Book production by Wiley Publishing, Inc. Composition Services
Wiley Bicentennial Logo: Richard J. Pacifico

About the Author

Steve Grenard is an avid herpetologist with more than forty years of experience with amphibians and reptiles; he published a paper on the reproduction of the Marsupial Frog in 1958. In the summer of 2000, he published a controversial and widely debated review in *Natural History Magazine* on the possibility of American rattlesnake venoms evolving new properties. He is the author of several Howell Book House titles, including: *Your Happy Healthy Pet: Bearded Dragon, An Owner's Guide to a Happy Healthy Pet: The Lizard,* and *Amphibians: Their Care and Keeping.* He is also the author of a number of scholarly medical and herpetological books, including *Medical Herpetology* and *Handbook of Alligators and Crocodiles,* and is the author of *Introduction to Respiratory Care,* a best-selling text review of respiratory therapy. Steve is a board-certified respiratory therapist and polysomnographer and is the clinical coordinator of the Institute of Sleep Medicine at Staten Island University Hospital in Staten Island, New York.

About Howell Book House

Since 1961, Howell Book House has been America's premier publisher of pet books. We're dedicated to companion animals and the people who love them, and our books reflect that commitment. Our stable of authors—training experts, veterinarians, breeders, and other authorities—is second to none. And we've won more Maxwell Awards from the Dog Writers Association of America than any other publisher.

As we head toward the half-century mark, we're more committed than ever to providing new and innovative books, along with the classics our readers have grown to love. From bringing home a new puppy to competing in advanced equestrian events, Howell has the titles that keep animal lovers coming back again and again.

Contents

Shopping List

You'll need to do a bit of stocking up before you bring your frog or toad home. Below is a basic list of must-have supplies. For more detailed information on the selection of each item below, consult chapter 4. For specific guidance on what food you'll need, review chapter 5.

For land or semiaquatic species:

☐ Tank with secure, partially vented top

☐ Substrate (sterile soil or small, rounded pebbles)

☐ Shallow water dishes

☐ Manual spray mister or automated system

☐ Thermometer

☐ Plants (ferns and other small terrestrial plants or hanging air plants)

☐ Water conditioners

☐ Hiding places, such as ceramic caves or PVC pipe

☐ Climbing places (for tree frogs) such as driftwood logs and branches

☐ Small plastic travel carrier

☐ Appropriate live food

For strictly aquatic species:

☐ Tank and stand

☐ Substrate (smooth gravel or pebbles)

☐ Tight-fitting glass hood or screen cover

☐ Inside box filter with air pump

☐ Water conditioner and pH test kits

☐ Submersible thermometer

☐ Floating island

☐ Aquatic plants

☐ Clean plastic bucket

☐ Nets

There are likely to be a few other items that you're dying to pick up before bringing your frog or toad home. Use the following blanks to note any additional items you'll be shopping for.

☐ _____

☐ _____

☐ _____

☐ _____

☐ _____

Pet Sitter's Guide

We can be reached at (___)_____-_____ Cell phone (___)_____-_____

_____

We will return on _____ (date) at _____ (approximate time)

Other individual to contact in case of emergency _____

_____

Number of frogs and toads we have, and species: _____

_____

Care Instructions

In the following blank lines, let the sitter know what to feed, how much, and when; what tasks need to be performed daily; and what weekly tasks they'll be responsible for.

Morning_____

_____

_____

_____

_____

Evening _____

_____

_____

_____

_____

_____

Other tasks and special instructions _____

_____

_____

_____

_____

_____

_____

Part I
All About Frogs and Toads

A Typical Frog

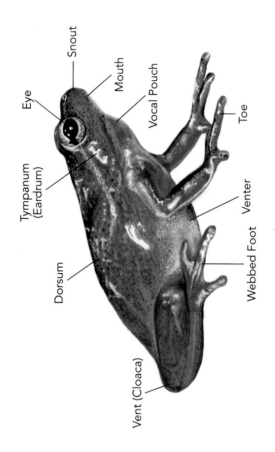

Snout

Eye

Mouth

Vocal Pouch

Toe

Tympanum
(Eardrum)

Venter

Dorsum

Webbed Foot

Vent (Cloaca)

Chapter 1

What Are Frogs and Toads?

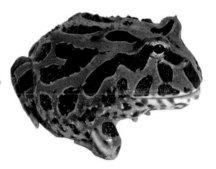

Frogs and toads are four-legged, tailless, air-breathing vertebrates that represent the link between the fish and reptiles and all other air-breathing species, including humans. They are members of a class or group of vertebrates known as the *Amphibia,* a word that means "dual life" and refers to the fact that amphibian life occurs in two phases—one in the water and the other on land. It also alludes to the fact that many amphibians are, well, amphibious, and are as fully at home in the water as they are on land (although there are many notable exceptions, including species that never leave the water and others that stay on land or in trees and never enter the water at all).

The first amphibians, the labryinthodonts, took the great leap from water to land during the Devonian period some 400 million years ago. However, fossils of frogs appear much later, in the Jurassic period of North America, some 280 million years ago.

The other amphibian groups or orders include the Caudates or Urodeles, which are known familiarly as salamanders and newts, and an obscure order known as the *Apoda* (legless amphibians), or caecilians. These segmented, wormlike creatures are found primarily in tropical regions and remain burrowed in moist soil most of the time. Little is known of their habits or life history.

Clearly, of all the amphibians, frogs and toads are the most familiar and best studied. Frogs and toads are members of the order *Anura,* a term that means "tailless," which is exactly what they are—bereft of a true tail, unlike their salamander cousins.

At the basic level, frogs and toads are tailless amphibians.

So Many Frogs and Toads

There are more than an estimated 5,200 species and subspecies of frogs and toads in the world, but nobody knows exactly how many there really are because new species and subspecies are being discovered by scientists at the rate of more than a dozen a year. Amazingly, it is predicted that such discoveries may go on indefinitely, as long as the precious habitats of these animals is protected from destruction. Environmental insults and habitat destruction have already caused the extinction of countless species over the last few decades; it is theorized that some rare species became extinct before scientists learned of their existence. Since 1980, at least 120 species of amphibians are believed to have become extinct, although there may be many more.

The number of different species of frogs and toads increases as the climate gets warmer, and the neotropical and tropical regions of the world tend to have more species than the temperate, and therefore colder, climates. In one small valley (San Cecilia) in Ecuador's Amazon basin, scientists discovered a total of eighty-one species of frogs and toads, finding fifty-six in just one night! This is all the more remarkable when you consider that there are about ninety frog and toad species in the whole United States.

Frogs and toads are an essential part of our ecosystem. Each individual animal consumes untold quantities of insect pests in a single day and helps to keep noxious insect populations in check. Without frogs and toads, the Earth would be overrun with crop-eating and disease-spreading bugs.

On the Brink

In February 2007, a group of amphibian biologists convened an extraordinary meeting in Atlanta, Georgia, to map a worldwide effort to save amphibian species from extinction. The scientists calculated that about a third of the world's 6,000 species of frogs and salamanders are at risk of extinction and at least 168 known species have already disappeared. The major threat that's killing amphibians worldwide is the disease chytridiomycosis, caused by the chytrid fungus (see chapter 8 for more on this deadly disease). Other threats include global warming, habitat lost to development, chemical pollution, and introduced fish species.

With the backing of the United Nations International Union for the Conservation of Nature, the scientists who make up the Conservation Breeding Specialist Group hope to establish a $500 million Amphibian Ark using zoos, public aquariums, and botanical gardens throughout the world to house and breed amphibians that are in danger of extinction.

Serious amphibian hobbyists can contribute to the effort not only by donating money to this project, but by publishing what they learn about *captive husbandry*—feeding, breeding, and raising frogs and salamanders in captivity. You can read about the findings and activities of Amphibian Ark at www.amphibianark.org.

Their existence also provides food for larger carnivores, including humans. Their *larvae,* or tadpoles, consume aquatic weeds that might otherwise clog up waterways. Clearly, frogs and toads play a vital role in the environment, and there is no telling what would happen if they suddenly all disappeared.

But disappearing they are. It is feared that frogs are declining in overall numbers, and some populations have completely vanished for reasons we do not yet understand. Even casual observers walking in wetlands they've visited for years are now finding that the frogs or toads that were once there are no longer present.

The decline in wild frog populations is alarming to environmentalists and frog lovers.

More alarming still is that this loss of wildlife is occurring even in seemingly pristine and untouched habitats. These declines baffle environmentalists, who hope that by studying frogs in captivity as well as in the wild they may one day solve these mysterious absences.

Classifying Frogs and Toads

The most basic units of any animal or plant classification system are the species and subspecies. And although there have been many efforts to precisely define what a species is, it is impossible to establish any firm rules that apply in every case. Members of a single species all look alike, live in a similar habitat, eat the same foods, and reproduce in the same manner, usually with one another. The exception is when two different species accidentally mate and produce a hybrid. Over time, if these hybrids survive and breed with one another, a new species is eventually created.

The American bullfrog's species name, *catesbeiana*, honors the pioneering British naturalist Mark Catesby (1683–1749). Catesby traveled to the New World to study the flora and fauna of the Americas. He wrote and published *The Natural History of Carolina, Florida and the Bahama Islands* in 1743.

Some animals are similar enough to be considered members of the same species, but there may be slight differences in different populations. This results in a subspecies category.

Above the species level, all animals that are very similar in general appearance are members of a genus, and above that they belong to a larger group called a family. These classifications are generally based on anatomical similarities.

Naming Species and Subspecies

Every species has a two-part Latin or Greek name and subspecies have a three-part name. The first part of the name is its genus, and the second part is its species. If there is a third part, it's the subspecies designation. Thus, the American bullfrog, with no known subspecies, is a member of the genus *Rana* and species *catesbeiana*. Its scientific name is written: *Rana catesbeiana*.

In the printed literature, scientific names are always italicized. The full classification of the American bullfrog is written as follows:

Phylum	*Chordata* (animals with a spinal cord)
Subphylum	*Vertebrata* (animals with a backbone or vertebral column)
Class	*Amphibia* (amphibians)
Family	*Ranidae* (the family of true frogs and riparian frogs)
Genus	*Rana* (the true frogs)
Species	*catesbeiana*

There are about forty-one families of frogs and toads, but only some of the best known, most interesting, and more commonly studied groups will be included in this book—although others will be briefly mentioned in chapter 7, which lists many species that may be kept as pets.

The Gifts of Frogs and Toads

Over the centuries there have been innumerable scientific discoveries made with the assistance of frogs and toads. They are among the first vertebrate species studied by future doctors and other scientists, and the sum total of all knowledge that people have garnered from the mere existence of frogs and toads is beyond calculation.

Recently, many species have been studied as a source of valuable new drugs, such as peptide antibiotics, painkillers, and even cancer-fighting agents. Scientists have only just touched the tip of the proverbial iceberg where this research is concerned.

There is much more to learn about frogs and toads, and, if they survive, they will undoubtedly continue to be a never-ending source of benefits to humans.

What's the Difference Between a Frog and a Toad?

The difference between a frog and a toad is actually more illusory than real. Both terms have been used interchangeably in different parts of the world. There are some generalizations that can be made about the way the terminology is used in the United States though.

First and foremost, all toads are frogs, but all frogs are not necessarily toads—although a few are. So regardless of whether you call a particular species a toad, it is still technically a frog.

In the United States, we tend to classify toads as mainly terrestrial or land-dwelling amphibians that enter the water only to breed and lay their eggs. We tend to think of frogs as aquatic or semiaquatic animals—equally at home in the water and on damp ground.

The problem with this definition is that there are frogs that never or rarely enter the water except to breed, such as the tree frogs—frogs that, as a rule, spend as much time as possible up in the trees and about as far away from water as you can imagine. On the other hand, there are species, such as the Surinam toad (*Pipa pipa*), that spend all their lives in the water and would quickly die if stranded on land. Yet, despite their strictly aquatic lifestyle, they somehow earned the name "toad."

Therefore, all you can say about this subject is to ask another question: "What's in a name?" The only rule about giving common names to frogs and toads is that there are no rules.

That's a southern toad on the left and a Florida gopher frog on the right. The difference between a frog and a toad is not always clear.

Chapter 2

Frog Anatomy

I f you were asked how to best describe the average frog, you would have to say that they have relatively broad bodies (although a few types are slimmer), no identifiable neck, no tail, and four legs. The rear legs are one and a half to three times longer than the front legs. The mouth is broad and sits below the snout at the front of the body. The other end of the gastrointestinal tract terminates in a structure known as the *cloaca,* through which both liquid and solid wastes pass, as well as eggs in females and sperm cells in males. The eyes are prominent orbs that sit at the top of the head. The frog skeleton looks very similar from one species to the next, although a trained eye can discern differences among various species.

Frogs and toads are *ectotherms,* which means they cannot produce their own internal body heat. Thus, they are constantly moving about, either to cool off or to warm up, because the temperature of their environment controls their body temperature.

Limbs and Locomotion

Frogs descended from their tailed predecessors, the salamanders, which waddle or scuttle along using all four legs in some sort of a rhythmic but seemingly discordant fashion. Frogs and toads improved on this form of locomotion by developing the ability to jump or, at worst, hop along at speeds that far exceed that of any terrestrial salamander.

The Unique American Tailed Frog

The American tailed frog (*Ascaphus truei*) is special in several ways. Nearly one-third of the tadpole's body length consists of the mouth, not counting the tail. The mouth is huge, rounded, and looks and works like a vacuum cleaner.

What's more, adult tailed frogs have no lungs and breathe only through their skin. Their lack of lungs also means they have no voice; so, unlike most frogs, they have to find other ways to locate mates. It is theorized that they sniff out potential mates using pheromones.

Some larger species can jump prodigious distances. In fact, some frogs can jump so fast and so far they have earned themselves the common name of rocket frog, and there are so many fantastic leapers among the frogs that it is difficult to decide which species are the best. In general, the Ranid or water frogs, such as the American bullfrog and its relative, the African giant bullfrog (*Conraua goliath*), are the species most often entered into frog-jumping contests. When it comes to getting around, the remarkable flying frogs of the genus *Rhacophorus* can actually glide from branch to branch in trees, holding onto branches with specially modified fingertips.

Although large Ranids such as the African giant bullfrog or Goliath frog are powerful jumpers, a frog's size is not often a factor in its ability to jump long distances. The tiny black-spotted tree frog (*Hyla nigromaculata*), which measures a scant 1.2 inches from the tip of its nose to its cloacal vent, can jump a distance of nearly 5 feet! And the smallish Carpathian frog (*Rana dalmatina*) has been measured jumping more than 9 feet.

Which is the slowest and clumsiest of frogs and toads is open to debate. Some argue that the large, heavy land toads (of the genus *Bufo*) that hop around in short bursts are the winners here. Others contend that the frogs known commonly as walking frogs, that are capable of getting around only by walking slowly and deliberately toward their objective, have the least impressive gait. These frogs are condemned to walking as a result of their poorly developed, though quite normal, hind limb musculature. Similarly, the narrow-mouthed toads (*Breviceps sp.*) crawl or creep around, at best.

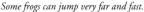
Some frogs can jump very far and fast.

Frog "Fingers"

Frogs and toads have four fingers, or front limb digits, and five hind limb digits, or toes. At least two species of frogs, the species *Chiroleptes platicephalus* and the tree frogs of the genus *Phyllomedusa,* have an opposable thumb. In aquatic and semiaquatic species there may be either slight or extensive webbing between the toes to facilitate swimming.

Nails or claws are unknown in frogs and toads, with three exceptions: the African clawed frogs (*Xenopus sp.* and *Silurana sp.*) and a burrowing species of toad known as *Rhinophrynus dorsalis.* The fingertips of these species have keratinized or thickened coverings that resemble nails or claws.

Frogs use their front legs, or "arms," to push food into and out of their mouths. They also use front and back legs to pull off old skin, which some stuff into their mouths.

Swimming

Most frogs are excellent swimmers. To propel themselves through the water, they use their hind legs exclusively, keeping their front limbs pressed against their sides. Aquatic and semiaquatic species have webbed hind feet, which increases

Not All Frogs Are Neckless

Although you would have a tough time locating the neck on most frogs, one group of five African frogs is an interesting exception to this rule. The snake-necked frogs (*Phrynomantis sp.*) have a clearly discernible neck that they can even turn side to side. This ability may not sound too impressive to us, but to a frog, this is quite a feat!

surface contact with the water and accelerates propulsion. The webbed feet of frogs served as inspiration for the flippers used by divers who, during World War II, were nicknamed "frogmen" as a testament to the animals that taught them how to swim efficiently underwater.

Frog Senses

Frogs and toads have the same sort of senses as other animals and people do: sight, hearing, smell, taste, and touch. In addition, their larvae (tadpoles) and some fully aquatic adult species have a *lateral line system* that is responsible for special senses needed for moving about underwater.

Sight

The eyes of frogs come in every conceivable color and pupil shape (round, vertical, horizontal, diamond-shaped), and they are one of the most unique and beautiful attributes of many species. The eyes of some species blend with facial and body coloration and patterns to make them a more difficult target for an attacker.

Bufonid toads have eyes that are flecked with gold and black; other toads' eyes are black with flecks of red or orange pigments. There are species with blue, green, and silver and gold eyes, as well. Most frogs have a mirrorlike layer of cells (called the tapetum lucidium) in the rear of their eyes that enables them to reflect light—an attribute known as eye-shine. This enables them to see better in very low light. If you cast a bright light around an area populated by frogs, their eye-shine will stand out in the pitch blackness of night.

The eyes of frogs are located in eye sockets mounted atop and on each side of the head. Frogs can see sideways and partially behind them, looking independently to the left and right with each eye. However, they have only a forty- to sixty-degree overlap in front, which gives them limited binocular vision.

The eyes of frogs come in just about every color and shape you can think of.

Frogs Can (Almost) See in Color

Frogs have some limited degree of color vision that favors the blue-green end of the spectrum. This is believed to be an adaptation that aids them when they need to escape, and they do so by leaping into the water, which is also at the blue end of the spectrum. "Head for the blue!" would be the warning cry of frogs in danger—unless they were tree frogs, in which case it would be, "Head for the green!"

Frogs use their eyesight to see the smallest movement of a possible prey item, and for this reason they are extremely farsighted—easily seeing objects fifty feet away but unable to focus on anything right under their nose. It is, in fact, their sense of smell that they use when a prey item is just about on top of them. The eyes retract down into their sockets when a frog or toad swallows its prey—the pressure exerted by the eyes during swallowing aids ingestion.

Underwater Vision

Frogs have movable eyelids and, in addition, a semitransparent, somewhat opaque, membranous eye cover called the *nictitating membrane.* This membrane protects the eyes when they need to be open under water. Vision, however, is clearly limited, and swimming frogs can probably see only shadows under the surface. Underwater, frogs are more likely to detect an object using their sense of smell rather than their vision.

Hearing

Frogs have an elaborate repertoire of vocalizations or calls that serve a variety of purposes, ranging from advertising for a mate to alerting others to danger (see "Frog Communication," page 113). But their voice would be of little use unless they had a first-class listening system to go along with it. All frogs and toads (with the exception of species in the genus *Bombina,* such as the Oriental fire-bellied toads) have a prominent external eardrum located slightly above and to the rear of their eyes. Sounds reaching the eardrum are conducted directly to the hearing structures located internally in back of it.

Frogs have no outer ear, although a few species have the vestiges of an outer earlobe or shell that serves to protect the tympanum (eardrum) as well as direct

Frogs have an elaborate repertoire of calls and keen hearing to interpret those calls.

the sound. The eardrum is prominent and easy to spot in large species such as the American bullfrog and its relatives, but in other species it is well disguised and has the same coloration as the head and body, making it difficult to see.

Frogs do not use their hearing to locate prey or sense danger. In one experiment, a chorus of calling frogs sitting in shallow water was subjected to the loud bang of a firecracker beyond their line of vision. They were unperturbed and continued to sing. However, a potential enemy that came into their line of sight caused them to retreat—as did the vibrations made on the surface of the water by slapping it with a canoe paddle. And while a warning or distress call uttered by a frog in imminent danger may cause all the other frogs in the area to go on red alert, it seems to take a lot more to elicit any activity from them. Frogs, therefore, seem to best use their hearing for making love, not war, and rely more heavily on the senses of sight, touch, and smell for feeding and detecting threats.

Smell

Frogs and toads unquestionably have a keen sense of smell that receives olfactory stimuli from at least two different sets of receptor organs—the conventional nasal passages and the vomeronasal organ (also known as the Jacobson's organ), located in the roof of the mouth. The *vomeronasal organ* consists of two fluid-filled sacs that connect to the nasal cavity via the nasopalatine ducts, and it processes scents in a different way than the nasal passages.

When a frog picks up the scent of food or danger, it is stimulated to search for it because the odor does not seem to pinpoint location so much as it merely indicates the presence in the general vicinity. The stronger the odor of a familiar substance, the greater the excitement level will be—whether odor detection of a predator, which dictates escape, or the sweet smell of a meal, which promotes frantic searching.

On detecting the odor of food, frogs will face in the general direction of the smell and begin to make grasping and mouth-opening movements. When the food item comes within about a quarter of an inch or less of the frog, its sense of smell tells the frog that a meal is at hand.

Frogs and toads in the water may also perceive a warning odor, given off by a wounded frog, toad, or tadpole nearby. It signals to the other frogs that a predator is around and that they should retreat and hide.

Although calling is the primary means by which frogs and toads find their mates, it is likely that odor and marking of territory also play some role in this behavior.

Scent is also used for navigating and spatial orientation. Frogs, given the choice of running a T-shaped maze with pure, distilled (no odor) water on one side and natural pond water on the other, invariably head for the pond water. Other species have been condi-

Smell is important in locating food and mates. When a frog smells food, it will orient toward the smell.

tioned to associate odors with various objectives in maze experiments, and such conditioning based on scent works extremely well. Some toads have learned to discriminate among a wide range of substances, including cedar balsam, creosote, and geranium oil.

It is also possible to confound the olfactory senses of frogs. In experiments with flies (which they love to eat) and a type of bug frogs loathe, researchers were able to confuse the frogs so badly that they ignored the flies when they should have been gobbling them up.

Taste

The taste buds of frogs and toads are embedded in the epithelium of the tongue and in the mucous membranes of the oral cavity. They sense the four basic taste categories: sweet, bitter, sour, and salty.

While they are less than discriminating in what they will eat, frogs do actively use their sense of taste to reject bugs and other prey items that do not taste just right to them. Their sense of taste helps them reject unwanted vegetable matter swept up in a feeding frenzy, as well as reject insects that may be poisonous to them. Frogs and toads will disgorge food matter that they find unpalatable without regard for table manners. They will even use their front legs to remove such items from their large mouths.

Touch

Frogs and toads appear to be sensitive to heat and cold, rough and smooth surfaces, and pain. Their sense of touch helps them avoid potentially harmful situations, and of all their sensory inputs, it is the most intimate, up close, and directly transmitted of the senses.

Lateral Line Organs: The Sixth Sense

Scientists believe that the lateral line organs or systems—a series of sensory canals under the skin along the sides that open to surface through special pores—exist as a special sixth sense on some animals, enabling them to sense water temperature conditions, water currents, and the existence of bioelectrical fields. Both marine and freshwater fish can detect galvanic signals (electric currents in the water) using their lateral line systems, although this ability is not proven in frogs and toads.

The lateral line system is present in almost all frog and toad tadpoles but disappears at metamorphosis. However, the strictly aquatic frogs, such as *Xenopus sp.* and *Pipa sp.* (including the African clawed frog and the Surinam toad), retain a lateral line organ system into adulthood, and it is believed to enable these animals to locate objects moving through the water in their vicinity. Because these frogs have small, practically useless eyes, this is an important compensatory sense that helps them navigate underwater.

Frog Skin

Not all frogs and toads are green, contrary to what most children brought up on heavy doses of Kermit and other cartoon frog characters are led to believe. In fact, frogs and toads run the gamut from green to browns, grays and bright colors, including red, yellow, blue, and purple. It is safe to say that somewhere, someplace, there is a frog with just about any color and pattern you can imagine.

Not all frogs are green. Dart-poison frogs are famous for their bright colors, which warn away predators.

Frogs that tend toward the greenish, brown, and gray ends of the color spectrum use their coloration for *crypsis,* which means blending in with their surroundings. This kind of camouflage helps prevent frogs from being eaten by predators. It also enables frogs to remain unseen as a prey item wanders into range.

Bright colors, such as reds and yellows, are known as *warning colors.* Species with these colors are advertising to potential predators that they are dangerous to eat because they will defend themselves with poisonous secretions.

Molting

Like all animals, frogs shed or *molt* their skin—some as often as daily. They do this by starting to eat it where it ends around their mouth. They use their legs and arms and contort their bodies to remove and push their loose skin toward the mouth, where they pull it in. Some frogs will dislodge pieces of their membranous epidermal layer, and you will find it floating around in their water bowl, lying in the corners of their enclosure, or smeared onto the glass walls of their aquarium.

Remove all dead skin by netting it up and flushing it down the toilet. Discarding uneaten pieces of molted skin is an important part of keeping your frog or toad's home hygienic, because the dead skin can provide an ideal medium for the culture of fungi and bacteria.

Sensitive Skin

Unlike fish, reptiles, birds, and mammals, amphibian skin has no scales, feathers, or hair to protect it. This makes amphibians unique. All of their skin must be kept moist to facilitate transcutaneous respiration and water absorption (both of which will be explained in the next section). The only real exception is the back of rough-skinned, leathery toads—they absorb water through the less leathery skin of their abdomen.

In addition, many species have skin that is heavily endowed with glands that produce both a protective layer of mucuslike material and a variety of proteins, alkaloids, and other poisonous or antibiotic substances. The mucous coat helps protect frogs from drying out or dehydrating, and their noxious secretions cause many predators to drop a frog or toad once they get a taste. Many predators are not likely to forget such an experience and tend to steer clear from ever trying to eat a frog or toad again, especially those that have warning colors, as previously mentioned.

Australian researchers have recently discovered an effective substance in frog skin that repels mosquitoes. They believe it holds great promise as a replacement for the controversial synthetic repellent DEET. Some problems need to be worked out before this substance becomes commercially available, such as the odor this new substance emits. And both its effectiveness and safety need to be thoroughly tested.

Water and Electrolyte Balance

Frogs and toads have a thin, membranelike permeable skin over all or most parts of their bodies. As a result, they rapidly absorb and excrete water and its constituents between their bodies and their environment. This includes electrolytes, in the form of mineral salts dissolved in their moist environment.

Frogs and toads also exchange gases (oxygen and carbon dioxide) through their skin in a process called transcutaneous respiration, and so they must keep all or a good part of their skin moist at all times. Even thick or leathery skinned bufonid toads have thinner skin on their underbelly and the undersides of their legs and rump, and they exchange water, electrolytes, and gases through parts of the body that are in contact with the substrate they are occupying.

Frogs and many toads are constantly in danger of dehydrating and dying if insufficient or no water is present in their environment—although a few species have adapted to arid conditions by digging well into the substrate to find moisture and remaining below until conditions at the surface improve.

The American spadefoot toads (*Scaphiopus sp.* and *Spea sp.*) are an excellent example. They know to dig their way out of their self-imposed subterranean cocoons when they hear raindrops hitting the surface above them. They rapidly do so, then breed and lay their eggs in temporary ponds or puddles. Their eggs and larvae develop quickly in these temporary bodies of water, and then the newly transformed frogs take a few meals and dig in again to await the next cycle of rain. Such species also develop extra layers of skin to keep them from drying out even if subterranean conditions become drier than usual. They can also tolerate dehydration to a far greater degree than other species. Spadefoot toads are estimated to be able to lose up to half of their total body weight in water without harm.

> **A Matter of Life and Death**
>
> Water supplied to captive frogs and toads should *always* be fresh water, treated to remove chlorine and to maintain normal pH for the species involved. Because frogs rapidly foul their captive aquatic environment, water should be vigorously filtered and/or changed frequently to remove noxious organic waste matter.

Temperature Regulation

Frogs and toads, like reptiles, fish, and all other amphibians, are ectothermic—they derive their body temperature from the temperature around them. Unlike birds and mammals, which produce their own heat metabolically, frogs and toads are completely dependent on their environment to regulate their internal body temperature.

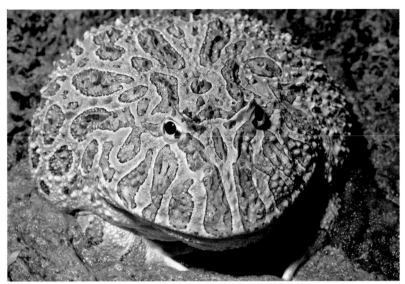

Frogs derive their body temperature from the temperature around them. Such animals are called ectotherms.

In nature, ectotherms regulate their body temperature by constantly moving from warmer to cooler spots, from sunny to shady areas, by burrowing into the substrate or diving into the water or emerging from it.

This has important implications for anyone keeping frogs or toads in a captive or unnatural environment. It is necessary, under such circumstances, to make sure you duplicate as closely as possible the external temperature variations of a particular species' natural environment. You can easily overheat a frog or toad with the result that it would stop eating, reduce or curtail its natural activity levels and, in extreme cases, quickly die as a result.

Generally, most amphibians prefer temperatures on the cooler side, as excessive warmth enhances the potential for evaporative dehydration. Tropical species that are used to

In addition to changing their environment, frogs also help to regulate their temperature by changing their skin color—lightening up to deflect heat and darkening to absorb it.

warmer temperatures must also be kept in containers with a high relative humidity. Dry heat under any circumstances is dangerous to just about all amphibians.

Chapter 3

Choosing Your Frog or Toad

Anumber of issues should dictate your choice of a first frog or toad. Your experience level with these types of pets is an important factor. It pays to start out with inexpensive, common species, and once you succeed with these for a year or more, it may be time to move on to rarer, prettier, more exotic, and more expensive frogs. (You'll find a long list of the types of toads and frogs available in chapter 7, along with some basic information about their individual care.)

Here in the United States you can readily find American bullfrogs, leopard frogs (*Rana pipiens*), green frogs (*Rana clamitans*), and a variety of common toads for sale in pet shops. A few more expensive and exotic species are not much more difficult to maintain than these common American species, however.

The South American horned frogs (*Ceratophrys sp.*) need little space in spite of their large size and will eat just about anything (graduating to small mice as they get larger). They move little and are content to sit and await prey. They have an amazingly beautiful mosaic coloration of green, gold, brown, and black. These frogs are considerably more costly than common U.S. species but are being bred in captivity. Even albinos are being bred, and their price is bound to drop as they become more plentiful.

Where to Get Your Frog or Toad

Local breeders and collectors, mail-order breeders and wholesalers, and local pet shops will all have frogs and toads for sale. Another way of acquiring frogs and toads is to attend swap meets and herp marts, which are held regularly all over the United States and in other countries. There are always a few frog and toad sellers there among the other reptile dealers.

Breeders

One of the best places to get a frog or toad is from a local breeder or *collector*—a person who breeds a small number of animals as a hobby. The advantages are numerous: Most hobby breeders are very conscientious about their animals and take great care in keeping and caring for them. Since the breeder has a wealth of experience in keeping and raising frogs, they will be able to answer any questions you have and pass on useful information and care tips. Price-wise, most hobby breeders are competitive with mail-order dealers, without the shipping costs.

There are a few disadvantages as well, and they must be carefully considered. The biggest problem in dealing with a hobby breeder is finding one. Even if you live in a large city, it is unlikely many frog breeders will live near you. And since few local breeders advertise, the only way to find them is through word of mouth. Your local herpetological society should be able to direct you to reputable breeders in your area—if there are any.

Another potential problem is variety. Breeding requires a lot of room and some expenditure of money. For this reason, most private breeders tend to specialize in one or, at most, a small number of species. And unless you are fortunate enough to find a person who breeds the species you are looking for, you may be out of luck.

Your first step is to decide what kind of frog you want and what kind of habitat you will be able to provide.

Before You Bring Your Frog Home

Before buying your frog, make sure that you are ready for it the minute you bring it through your door. A checklist may help:

☐ Housing setup ready and waiting, including lighting, temperature, humidity, and rainmaking or misting equipment. (In a pinch, a plant mister bottle can be used for a few days while you are waiting for the automated equipment to arrive from your mail-order purchase.)
☐ Handling and first aid equipment on hand.
☐ A small supply of live food on hand and a reliable steady source established in advance.
☐ A few gallon jugs of aged, chlorine-free tap water or natural spring water on hand.

Mail Order

If you cannot find interesting frogs for your collection locally, you can buy them by mail order. You can track down breeders and importers of interesting frogs by reading the popular magazines about reptiles and amphibians and contacting their advertisers. Breeders can also be found through local herpetological societies, and commercial dealers can be found on the Internet by doing a search for the keywords *frog breeder* or *frog prices*. (You'll also find some breeders listed in the appendix.)

The first step in obtaining a frog by mail order is to decide what species you would like. Then contact the dealer for a price list and to find out if they have the species you want.

Frogs are hardy creatures, so shipping them is not difficult. Most dealers will place your frog inside a cloth bag or a plastic container, along with some moistened paper towels or moss to keep it hydrated and as padding to prevent it from being bounced around. This container is

This Rana frog is easy to obtain, but the albino coloration is not as common. If you are seeking unusual frogs, or common frogs in unusual colors, mail order may be your best source.

then placed inside a shipping box, with several inches of newspaper or foam peanuts as insulation and padding, and the shipping box is completely sealed with tape to prevent rapid temperature changes. The box will then be marked "Live Frogs." There is enough air inside the box for several weeks, although most frogs reach their destinations overnight or within a few days.

You should specifically request that the shipping company require a signature from you upon delivery. This prevents the delivery person from simply leaving the box by your front door, where it may be exposed to direct sunlight and become too hot for your frog or chilly weather that is too cold for your frog.

When your pet arrives, it will be a bit disoriented by the trip, so you should remove it gently from the packaging, place it in the artificial habitat you set up, make sure there is food and water, and then leave it alone for a few days to adjust to its new surroundings.

Pet Stores

One big advantage a local pet store has over a mail-order dealer is that you are able to closely examine the frogs before you buy them. If you are able to find a frog you want in a pet store, take the opportunity to examine it carefully. Choosing a healthy frog to begin with will save you a lot of problems, heartache, and expense down the road.

A good pet store should be able to point you to the local herpetological society for help and advice concerning your frog or toad.

Choosing a Healthy Frog

Regardless of what frog you choose, make sure that its holding tank at the pet shop or other animal dealer is clean, that the animal's skin is normally colored (not too dark and not too light), and that it does not show any obvious signs of deformity.

Once you definitely decide you are going to buy a frog, ask for one final test—to see it eat. If the dealer has no food to feed it or otherwise refuses, you might think twice about how this frog has been maintained. If the frog does not eat or shows difficulty in eating, this may indicate that the frog has a serious problem that you don't want to take on.

Wild Caught vs. Captive Bred

It may seem like the easiest way to get a pet frog is to go to the local pond and catch one. But as the number of people enjoying the hobby of keeping frogs and toads has grown, so, too, have the pressures exerted upon native populations of

Signs of a Healthy Frog

- Good appetite
- Eyes open and alert
- Normal coloration (not too dark and not too light)
- Appropriate skin texture
- Hops when gently prodded
- Normal hopping and leaping
- Plump and hearty appearance

frogs and toads by collectors who capture wild amphibians for the pet trade. This only adds to the already crushing problems of loss of habitat and environmental pollution.

It's best if you're a beginner to stick with the widely available captive-bred species until you have enough experience and know-how to properly care for the rarer wild-caught animals. But even the most experienced keepers of frogs and toads should seek out and obtain captive-bred animals whenever possible, and should make every effort to avoid collecting any specimens of any species that have been taken from the wild.

These baby albino clawed frogs are banned in California. When nonnative species escape into the wild, they can overbreed and threaten native populations of animals.

Legal Issues

There are also some legal issues you must consider before you capture any wild frog or toad. Local collecting may be against the law; taking a frog or toad out of a local park in New York City, for example, is strictly forbidden. In many states, some species of frogs are protected as endangered species. Where they are not endangered, they are still subject to hunting and fishing regulations that prohibit their collection

Collecting frogs from the wild may seem easier than buying them. But there are environmental and legal issues to consider.

during certain times of the year, and they are also subject to bag and size limits in many jurisdictions. In some areas, fishing licenses are needed.

Strangely, a lot of states classify frogs as fish for the purposes of game regulation (this is probably just for the sake of expediency), and while this is clearly scientifically inaccurate, it benefits frogs in the same way fishing regulations protect fish stocks. (Frog-lovers, however, are incensed by the idea of categorizing frogs as fish and are lobbying for changes so that their special status can be appreciated.) Therefore, before you go out and collect some local frogs for pets, it's a good idea to first check your local regulations to avoid the possibility of getting a fine and a summons to appear in court.

There are no known local laws in the United States that prohibit the keeping of frogs in general, but there are some specific exceptions. The highly aquatic African clawed frog, for example, is banned in the state of California. This popular aquarium pet and laboratory frog has been accidentally released in some California waters, where it has established reproducing populations that concern California environmentalists. These frogs are not native members of the state's ecosystem, and they are harming native species, either by competing with them for food or by eating them. Before the situation grew any worse, California took the step of banning these frogs from the state except by special permit, and such permits are granted only to legitimate medical and scientific research facilities. African clawed frogs in California are treated almost like a deadly plague and are subject to strict controls where their licensed use is involved.

For more information about frogs, toads, and the law, see chapter 8.

Part II
Caring for Frogs and Toads

Chapter 4

Housing Your Frog or Toad

Appropriate housing for your frogs and toads is one of your most important considerations. Put a lot of thought and planning into your pet's housing, because frogs and toads don't easily tolerate less-than-ideal environments. Your first step is to decide what type of frogs or toads you want, and then to learn about their specific housing requirements.

Some totally aquatic species do well in an ordinary aquarium setup and others can be kept in a tank of shallow water with a few smooth rocks for them to climb out on. The more elaborate and decorative your setup, the more work it will be to tear down and clean. If you choose to have a very decorative setup, you should consider keeping only a very few small species to minimize the time and labor involved. You may be able to keep a few small species in a large vivarium for weeks, a month, or even longer with a minimum of maintenance. Larger toads and water frogs, however, are best housed in more spartan surroundings for the sake of cleanliness and convenience.

Give serious thought as to how you will keep the water clean. Aquariums containing the larger species or crowded with a number of frogs rapidly become fouled with their excreta. It may be necessary to set aside time each day or every two or three days to move the frogs to a temporary holding tank, change and clean the primary tank, and then put them back in their regular home.

Also make sure that you have the minimal facilities for the tasks you must perform. Dirty tank water should be flushed down the toilet or, alternatively, used to fertilize a flower bed (if you have one), and clean, aged (that is, dechlorinated) water should always be available to replace it.

The most convenient housing to use for any amphibian is a store-bought, all-glass aquarium tank. Pick a size that will not overcrowd your frogs. Make sure you get a screen cover rather than a glass top, because a glass cover will cause the air to stagnate, heat and humidity will build up, and microorganisms will flourish. It is better to keep the enclosure well ventilated and provide humidity from an external source regularly or as needed.

Terrariums for Land Dwellers

Tree frogs and mainly terrestrial species, such as most toads, require a *terrarium* consisting of a dry or land portion and perhaps just a small pond made out of a plastic food storage dish of suitable size. If you are keeping tree frogs and you wish to plant the tank for them, you need a tank that is high as well as wide and long. Use only sterile potting soil and sphagnum moss to lay down a layer of substrate for the plants.

The size of the tank will vary with the species you keep. No one rule or recommendation fits all. Tank size requirements for individual species are discussed in chapter 7.

A single small animal could be kept in a clear plastic box with a fitted screen cover, which is available in many pet shops. The drawback to plastic is that over time it becomes scratched, clouded, and discolored. Glass can be cleaned more easily with no risk of surface damage, unless you outright break it.

Terrestrial species need a tank with some branches to climb on and a water dish to soak in.

Your frog will appreciate having some hiding spots in its habitat.

Professional breeders and keepers who have no desire to attractively display their animals use utilitarian plastic bowls and dishes commonly available in supermarkets and large discount department stores. These dishes come in every size, shape, and height imaginable and often come complete with a fitted lid that can be drilled to provide air holes and circulation.

However, if you are going to display your frogs, an all-glass aquarium tank with a fitted screen lid is your best option. You are limited in size and shape options to mainly rectangular or hexagonal tanks that come in a variety of predetermined widths, lengths, and heights, depending on the gallon size you want. It may be possible for your pet shop to order a special size tank that is custom built to your specifications—but be prepared to pay for it. For example, you may want to house a number of frogs over a wide bottom surface area, but do not need the extra height of larger-size standard aquariums. On the other hand, you may want significant extra height for tree-dwelling species but may not require the larger surface area of ready-made fish tanks of that height.

If you wish to establish a decorative terrarium for your frogs, you should begin with a layer of coarse pebbles on the bottom, covered by sterile potting soil. Plant the soil with the plants you have chosen, making sure none of them are poisonous to your thin-skinned frogs or the insects they eat. Then cover the surface with a layer of orchid tree bark to hold down the soil. The problem with a highly decorated and planted terrarium is that some boisterous species will fling dirt up onto the glass, uproot plants or crush them, and in general make maintenance difficult. If you are considering such a jungle setup, think about keeping smaller, more delicate species of frogs that would be less likely to make a mess. Horned frogs, American bullfrogs, and marine or cane toads are a few of the large, active, or boisterous species that could throw a carefully planted tank into disarray. Smaller species, such as dart-poison frogs and mantellas, are daintier and better behaved.

Branches for Tree Frogs

Tree frogs have special housing needs. They can be kept in simple enclosures with paper towel substrate, as long as they are furnished with branches or pieces of high driftwood on which to climb. They can also be accommodated in more

Tree frogs need plants and branches to climb on.

elaborate planted terrariums, but bear in mind that their weight may damage all but the strongest or heaviest-stemmed varieties of live plants. They could also be provided with artificial plants or branches that can be removed, rinsed with plain water, and wiped down as necessary.

Ground Cover

If you want to use a substrate or ground cover, do not buy gravel or pebbles with sharp or angular edges. Thin-skinned frogs will easily scrape themselves on this material; such wounds can become infected and ultimately your animals could die. Decorative substrate should be smooth, water-worn pebbles. The same principle applies to rock formations: Avoid any sharp, jagged, or angular edges. All ridges and edges should be smooth to prevent cuts and abrasions.

Many experienced frog and toad keepers find that a layer of damp, plain white paper towel is the best material to use as a substrate. It is easy to see any soiling, and paper towels can be picked up, discarded, and replaced easily. This makes the chore of cleaning and maintaining hygienic conditions far simpler than if you use gravel, pebbles, sphagnum moss, or soil.

Atop the substrate place a plastic bowl, such as a food storage dish, with water in it for the frogs to soak or swim. Frogs and toads love taking baths. A "pond" made from a water bowl could take up half to one-third of the space on the floor of the tank, but both the tank and the pond must be large enough for your frogs or toads to sit down inside them.

If you're keeping small frogs, make sure the water is shallow enough for the frogs to sit in it without their heads being underwater and that they can easily climb out. Frogs can drown! It may be necessary to give them "steps" in the form of small stones or rocks for this purpose. The water catch trays used under flower-pots are excellent for this purpose, as are a wide variety of semidisposable plastic containers you can find in supermarkets.

Paper towels will *not* work for burrowing species, such as spadefoot toads and narrowmouthed toads. They need a sterile soil substrate of sufficient depth to

Make sure the water dish is shallow enough that the frog can get out. Adding steps or a small ramp may be the best way to keep your pet safe.

meet their natural requirements. Avoid silica sand and sharp, jagged-edge gravel; these substrates can irritate or even cut or abrade these thin-skinned species as they do what comes naturally for them—which is dig down and bury themselves. Spadefoot toads and other burrowing species will not be happy with pebbles either, so soil is your best bet for these kinds of frogs and toads.

We're not talking about ordinary backyard or garden dirt. This may contain traces of insecticides, bacteria, or contaminants, or noxious bugs that you do not want in contact with your frogs or toads. Use only store-bought sterile potting soil.

Substitute Sunlight

Most frogs and toads do not bask. They shun light, especially light that produces heat. They do not require exposure to UV light for bone growth, the way lizards do. In fact, adding such light for most species of frogs and toads may actually be harmful.

However, fire-bellied toads, mantellas, and the dart-poison frogs do need full-spectrum lighting to help bolster normal bone development and growth. These species have been observed basking in sunlight in the wild. Natural sunlight contains the full UV spectrum. Sunlight coming in through a window is not sufficient for animals that need full-spectrum lighting. What they need is a reptile light—a fluorescent tube or fixture that gives off light in the UV range. They are available at pet supply stores that sell reptiles.

If you add any lighting to your frog's home, do not leave it on twenty-four hours a day. Be sure to allow at least eight to twelve hours with no artificial lighting and some darkness. This is true for terrestrial, aquatic, and semiaquatic frogs and toads. Some species use the cover of darkness to rest, others are active during this period and rest by hiding during the lighted part of the day, and some frogs are active during periods of low light such as at dusk and dawn.

Aquariums for Aquatic Frogs

Strictly aquatic species are best kept in aquarium tanks. The African clawed frogs (*Xenopus sp.*) and the Surinam (*Pipa pipa*) toad are examples of strictly aquatic species that never come up on land. They are strong swimmers. They float at the surface to breathe but then dive and swim around more or less as if they were fish.

A setup for an aquatic frog or toad should mirror any tropical fish setup. It can have an under-gravel and an external power filter or a submersible box filter or a sponge filter, all of which are available in aquarium supply shops. The water will be sufficiently aerated with a good filter or multiple filter systems, so a separate airstone is not necessary.

It is important to make sure the aquarium is large enough to house the number of frogs you are keeping and to accommodate their size. The more frogs, the greater the aquarium size required. A good basic rule is about half an inch of frog per gallon, with a minimum size of ten gallons. Thus, a ten-gallon tank could comfortably hold five 1-inch frogs or one 5-inch frog.

You'll need a screen cover with a light mounted above it, if desired, for viewing, and some aquatic plants and other decorative items. If you're using lights, they should be fluorescents that do not give off much heat—remember, they are for the viewing convenience of humans, not the frogs. Aquatic frogs prefer temperatures in the high 60s to mid-70s Fahrenheit. A heater is not required unless

An aquarium for an aquatic frog should mirror the conditions of pond life.

> **TIP**
>
> Keeping frogs of different sizes together in the same enclosure fosters the likelihood of the larger frogs eating the smaller ones, so this housing arrangement should be avoided.

the water is apt to cool below 70 degrees. Use a thermometer made for fish tanks to periodically check the water temperature.

Some mostly aquatic frogs like to haul out onto floating islands that you can buy, which are typically made of aquarium-safe cork or Styrofoam. African clawed frogs and Surinam toads don't require these, because they never come out of the water.

Plants or aqua-safe caves and other hiding places are recommended, because frogs don't always like to be out in the open. Larger clawed frogs and Surinam toads will uproot plants, so a sparse tank arrangement is recommended for these frogs. For them, caves and rock formations of sufficient size can be placed in the tank as hiding places.

Taking Care of the Tank

This kind of tank will require the same kind of maintenance as a fish tank, and how often you clean it depends on how powerful the filter is and how rapidly it gets dirty. Obviously, the greater the number of frogs you keep in a single aquarium, the faster it will become fouled. Remember, too, that frogs create more of a *bioload*—they get the tank dirtier—than typical aquarium fish, so you will need powerful filtration and frequent cleaning for your tank. Use an Aqua-Vac or similar device to clean out gross particulate matter, such as shed skin and fecal material.

The pH of your aquatic frog's water should be kept from 6.5 to 7.0, so you'll need a pH test kit for this. The water is apt to become increasingly acidified (below pH 7.0) by urinary and fecal wastes, so partial water changes will be needed to maintain the pH at safe levels. (A pH of 7.0 is neutral. If the pH drifts above 7 it becomes alkaline; if it goes below 7 it becomes acidic.)

Aqua-Terrariums for Semiaquatic Frogs

The aqua-terrarium is for *semiaquatic frogs*—those that need both a place to swim and some dry land—and there are a number of strategies for meeting the needs of these species. Semiaquatic frogs include most of the Ranid species and such popular pet frogs as the Oriental fire-bellied toad (yes, another frog called a toad). The same rule, half an inch of frog per gallon of tank, also applies to semiaquatic species.

A Word About Quarantine

Many experts believe that all new frogs and toads brought into an existing collection should be quarantined in a separate holding tank, preferably located in a separate room or as far from existing animals as possible. The function for quarantine is to prevent the newcomers from spreading any diseases to healthy frogs and toads in your collection.

Whether quarantine for new arrivals is absolutely necessary for frogs and toads is a matter of debate among veterinary specialists. However, it cannot hurt, and all new frogs might best be observed in isolation for a week or so before coming into proximity with your existing pet frogs.

Using a regular aquarium tank, you can slope several pounds of gravel against one side and add water to the other, creating, in effect, a pool and a beach. A more elaborate plan is to have a piece of glass or acrylic cut to size and divide the tank into a land side and a water side. The land side could be created by filling that half of the tank with smooth pea gravel or water-worn pebbles. Soil is not recommended, as it would soon turn to mud. The "beach" slope should be gradual so your frog can easily get out of the water.

Another way of providing for semiaquatic species is to fill a large (20 gallons or more) aquarium with water to a depth of 3 to 5 inches and then add good-sized rocks with ridges on them in the middle or at the ends so the frogs can haul out on to them. The rocks must rest on the bottom and extend at least ½ inch to 1 inch above the water level. A layer of pebbles should line the bottom of the tank to prevent the rocks from cracking the bottom. This setup has the effect of creating an island for your frogs with water all around it or to one side, depending on where you place the rocks.

A few companies make ready-made pools, stoneware, and even small, air-pump powered waterfalls that you can insert into your frog setup, greatly enhancing its appearance and making it more homey for its occupants.

Any of the setups mentioned here can also be used with external background scenes, insertable cork, molded plastic, or foam backgrounds to help decorate the enclosure. These are available in most aquarium supply shops and are made

Semiaquatic species need a tank that is part water and part land.

to fit the standard-size aquarium tanks. These trappings are a matter of individual taste.

You'll need a small dish for a soaking pond. Food dishes are optional, since most bugs crawl out of them and frogs like to hunt around their enclosure for a meal. A humidity gauge is another optional piece of equipment for the few species that live in very humid environments.

Frogs love to hide, so safe hiding places are *not* optional. Hiding places can be made of artificial logs. Caves and rock formations made of ceramics and other safe materials are available in pet supply shops. Although not as pretty, some pros simply use lengths of 2-inch diameter plastic pipe.

You'll also need a water conditioner for dechlorinating water.

In all these setups, you need to siphon out the water at least once every two days and replace it with clean water (see "Like Water for Frogs," below). If you completely change the water daily you may not need a filtration system, but that depends on just how dirty the water gets in between changes. Having a filter is a good back-up in case you miss a water change.

Like Water for Frogs

Water quality is vitally important for frogs (see chapter 2 for more on why that is so). Although some species may live in brackish, acidic, or highly alkaline waters, captive frogs, with few exceptions, can be safely maintained in water with a neutral pH (7.0). Fecal wastes and urine rapidly acidify frog water, so it must be either filtered vigorously or changed frequently.

If you are using tap water, it should be aged for a day or two so that chlorine dissipates. Tap water is normally aged by letting it sit in an open container for twenty-four hours. This allows the chlorine to vaporize and dissipate. If you decide to use bottled water, it is better not to use pure distilled water because distilled water lacks trace elements and minerals that can benefit frogs.

Therefore, if you buy your frog water, it is worthwhile to choose mineral spring waters. Naturally, do not use any "designer" waters that are lightly flavored with various fruits or mint! And frogs are not likely to appreciate the tiny bubbles of seltzer either—although carbonated water can be used in an emergency for water bowl refills. Strictly aquatic frogs may be overwhelmed by the bubbles of carbon dioxide in bubbly water, so it should be avoided for aquatic species.

Rain

Frogs and toads love rain, and rain is an important factor in stimulating them to mate and breed. Whether you intend to breed your frogs or simply intend to duplicate natural rain or mist several times a day, you may want to invest in a timer-controlled rainmaking system. This system comes with a reservoir, a water pump, and a network of small plastic piping and nozzles through which water is forced under pressure. Aimed into your tank (through a tiny hole cut into the screen cover), you can literally make it rain on your frogs and toads, even if only for a short period. Torrential downpours should be avoided, as the water really has no place to go once your substrate becomes saturated.

Or you can manually rain on your frog's parade by using a plant mister on them for a few minutes each day. Set aside a separate mister that you use only for the frogs, so you know that nothing but water will ever be poured into the bottle.

Frogs and toad love rain. You can get automatic misting equipment, or be a personal rainmaker for them every day.

Water Essentials

- Water is vital for the life of your frogs. Frogs exchange essential electrolytes and gases through their skin. A dehydrated frog will rapidly die. The substrate should be damp to the touch but not wringing wet. Misting for 10 to 15 seconds daily helps maintain this moisture level. Keeping the tank partially covered with glass holds in the moisture, but some air should be allowed to circulate.
- Water should always be kept clean. Filtration systems help maintain clean water, but partial or complete water changes every other day (or a minimum of three times a week) are critical.
- Remember that the more frogs you keep in a given volume of water, the faster it will get dirty. Enlarging the size of your enclosure or cleaning it more frequently are your primary options. You might also trade or sell a few frogs—if you can bear to part with them.
- Although frogs and toads need water, small frogs and baby frogs can and do drown. If you're keeping small frogs, make sure whatever setup you have allows them to easily haul out of the water and to sit in the water with their rumps on the bottom, keeping their heads above water. Call it a kiddie pool.

Special Water Conditions

Some species prefer special water conditions. Research your frog's special needs and do as much as you can to meet them. If you do not know the needs of your particular frogs, a pH of 7.0 is safest. You'll need a pH test kit to check your local water. These are available at aquarium supply stores. You can also buy natural chemicals (again, designed for aquarium fish) to lower the pH of your water.

Heavy metals are often-overlooked water contaminants that can impair or even kill your frogs. Poisoning from these metals is often slow and insidious and little can be done to reverse it. Many plumbing systems may leech trace amounts of copper, lead, or zinc into the water. You can combat this by allowing the tap to run for several minutes before setting aside water to age. This flushes away any dissolved metals in the first spurts of water.

Recent research indicates that agricultural pesticide contamination is causing limb deformities and even missing limbs in frogs and toads as they develop from tadpoles into adults. Cases of extra limbs forming have also been observed.

A Benefit of Tap Water

On occasion, frogs with skin infections or fungal growths have been successfully treated by maintaining them in chlorinated tap water for short periods; check with an experienced veterinarian about this. This practice may be worth trying if you encounter these kinds of problems that might otherwise be ultimately fatal. (Treating the medical problems of frogs is covered in more detail in chapter 6.)

Frogs that metamorphose with three rear legs are at a disadvantage because they are highly uncoordinated; this results in a disability that makes it difficult for them to capture food or escape from predators.

Temperature Control

Most frogs and toads prefer moderate, cooler temperatures ranging from the mid-60s to the mid-70s Fahrenheit. Excessive heat, especially coupled with dryness, causes them to rapidly dehydrate and die. For this reason, many species of frogs and toads are active only at dawn, dusk, or night. During the hottest parts of the day, most are hiding somewhere, staying cool. Even tropical species from hot countries in South America, Africa, and Asia arrange their daily schedules to be active when temperatures drop into the low 80s or the 70s Fahrenheit.

Be mindful that even if your frog is from an area where the noonday temperatures reach 100 degrees Fahrenheit or more, that does not mean it likes it that way. Nighttime temperatures may drop 20 degrees or more, and this is when your frog is likely to be most active. The descriptions of species in chapter 7 will offer some temperature range guidelines, where this information is known. Finding out where your frog lives in nature and researching temperatures in these areas is one way you can determine for yourself what temperature ranges your frog or toad likes best.

It is necessary to accommodate the temperature needs of your frogs and toads. Glass aquariums used to house frogs and toads should never be sealed on top with a piece of glass or acrylic, as this will cause heat to be retained and to build up. A tight-fitting, locking-type screen cover that keeps your frogs from jumping or climbing out is best.

Most frogs, even those from hot climates, prefer moderate temperatures.

In the hot summer months, you may have to find a cool place to keep your frog tank, even if it means using an air conditioner or household climate control system all the time. In the cold months, if you allow your household temperatures to drop below 70 degrees Fahrenheit, most frogs will become inactive. You may have to use an undertank heating pad under a part of their enclosure during this period. You can also warm a part of the tank using a low-wattage incandescent lighting fixture and bulb. These bulbs are also available in red and blue for nighttime heating use. (Make sure a part of the tank always remains unheated, so your pet can move away and cool down.)

For aquatic setups, a submersible aquarium heater and a thermometer is the best option for making sure the water doesn't get too cold.

Hot rocks, which are sold for warming reptile enclosures, should never be used in a frog tank. The danger of electrical shock in a damp environment is simply too great. Moreover, use of these devices poses a serious threat of thermal burns to the delicate skin of frogs and toads.

Finally, you should also invest in a good quality thermometer that you can place in the tank temporarily to take a reading. If it is too hot (over 82 degrees Fahrenheit) or too cold (under 65 degrees Fahrenheit), modify the situation accordingly. In emergency overheating situations, it can help to set up an electric fan and aim it at your frog tank for the duration of the heat spell. The circulation will help dissipate heat from the tank.

Chapter 5

Feeding Your Frog or Toad

When describing the food and feeding habits of any animal, it is helpful to know the language that is used to characterize these habits. So let's start with the basics: Carnivores eat animal protein, including insects; herbivores eat vegetable matter; and omnivores eat both animal and vegetable matter.

Frog and toad larvae or tadpoles are either carnivorous, omnivorous, or, rarely, herbivorous, depending on the species. All adult frogs and toads are carnivorous, with the majority more accurately described as insectivores, or insect eaters. (Although a vegetarian species of adult frog has recently been reported, it may eat vegetable matter serendipitously rather than deliberately.) Larger species will consume other types of animal matter, including arthropods other than insects (for example, crayfish), fish, and small mammals such as mice, small birds, small snakes, and lizards. Some species will even eat other frogs and toads, including members of their own species—which makes them cannibals.

The vast majority of all frogs and toads are stimulated to eat by sighting movement in their food. They do not consume dead or inanimate insects or animal matter, although a few species of toads have been observed eating dog food left outside for Rover. One technique you can try when feeding dead prey to frogs is to wiggle it around in front of them, perhaps with a stick or other object, to stimulate the frog to eat.

Insects

It is best to feed *live* insects, such as crickets, fruit flies, spiders, earthworms, moths, or other living creatures—because, as just mentioned, motion is what stimulates frogs to eat. Just toss them in the tank and let your pet hunt.

Live insects are best because the motion of the insect stimulates the frog to eat.

The first questions you should ask the pet shop owner or dealer before you buy a frog or toad are what they have been feeding it and if they can assure you that they will always be stocking this food. Many pet shops that sell frogs and toads also carry feeder insects, and this is an ideal source of food for these animals in small, conveniently priced purchases when you need them. You may be able to obtain enough food on each visit to feed your animals for several days to a week.

If your pet shop cannot supply you year-round with the appropriate live foods for your frogs, you will have to consider bringing them in by mail order. (A list of some live insect and small mammal providers is included in the appendix.)

You may want to consider co-oping large feeder insect shipments with other frog fanciers in your area, especially if you find that frequently purchasing small quantities from the local pet shop is getting expensive. Just remember that you will have to store the live insects—and keep them well fed and healthy.

Some fanciers decide to raise their own feeder insects. There is a lot of information about this on the Internet, and you can buy kits to get you started. When the season permits, you can also collect your own bugs. Make sure you do this only from areas that have not been treated with pesticides, herbicides, fertilizers, and other potentially harmful chemicals.

They're Not Picky Eaters

All species of frogs or toads will eat bugs of any kind: crickets, springtails, moths, worms, mealworms, super mealworms, ants, flies, and termites, to name just a few. Larger frogs can be fed newborn and fuzzy mice, and a few really big species will gobble up fully grown mice. Frogs and toads are fairly indiscriminate eaters. If they really don't like a food item, they'll try it anyway and then spit it out. If this is the response, take that item off your list.

Regardless of how you choose to feed your frogs or toads, be sure you budget appropriately for the feeding and upkeep costs, or you will soon lose them.

Gut-Loading

The best way to make sure the food you feed your pets is nutritious is by a process called gut-loading. It involves feeding the food insects a very healthy diet—or at least dusting them with vitamin and mineral supplements formulated for this purpose, which are available in pet supply shops. You also gut-load such creatures as mealworms and crickets

> **What About Water?**
>
> Adult frogs and toads obtain water almost exclusively by absorbing it through their skin, so they must have opportunities to soak in water bowls or absorb moisture from the substrate.

by dusting a piece of raw potato or carrot with extra vitamins and dropping this enriched food into the enclosure used to house the bugs or mealworm larvae.

How Much Food?

Given the right temperature and humidity conditions, a healthy frog or toad is a voracious eater and needs to be fed at least every other day. A few smaller species require copious quantities of tiny insects daily or every other day. If three days go by

Some frogs are naturally big and fat, but you must still resist the temptation to overfeed them. This White's tree frog can become blind from overfeeding.

Don't Overfeed Your Frogs

Overfeeding large carnivorous species, such as horned frogs, marine toads, and bullfrogs, especially with small mammals such as mice or rat pups, can cause obesity and in some cases a buildup of fatty plaque. In fact, this type of diet has been blamed for blindness in the White's tree frog (*Litoria caerulea*), a popular large pet species. Keep an eye on your frogs and toads to make sure they don't get too plump.

---

without feeding them, these animals can die of starvation. This obviously causes logistical problems if you are thinking about owning frogs, because you must ensure a steady food supply even during the winter months, when feeder insect shipments are apt to arrive dead or dying from exposure to the cold.

Food is also an important financial consideration. The costs of feeding a hungry frog can quickly mount, and over the months and years the cost of the food is apt to far exceed the original cost of the animal. The same can be said, of course, about any pet—the maintenance costs often surpass the acquisition cost—but many people forget to consider this at the outset.

Feeding Tadpoles

Most of the time, raising and feeding tadpoles is an infinitely simple affair. Vegetarian or omnivorous species (remember, they're only vegetarians when they're juveniles) can be fed small pieces of boiled lettuce, aquarium plants such as Elodea and others commonly available in aquarium supply shops, and, occasionally, pieces of boiled spinach. (Although spinach has many important nutrients to help your tadpoles grow, it also contains substances that can cause kidney problems in tadpoles so it should not be given except in small amounts and no more than once a week.) Lighting their tank will also cause the growth of algae, which some types of tadpoles relish, and quite a few species will readily eat vegetarian fish food flakes of appropriate size.

Carnivorous or omnivorous tadpoles can also be fed regular tropical fish food flakes—the kind made from fish matter—and a variety of live fish foods, such as daphnia, strained brine shrimp, and aquatic worms. Many species of tadpoles will attack and feed on weaker or dead brothers and sisters, as well.

Tadpoles may be vegetarians or omnivores, but all adult frogs are carnivores.

The tadpoles of some of the dart-poison frogs are more difficult to feed and need to be isolated in small containers and carefully fed a drop or two of egg yolk from an eye dropper every day. Although this is labor-intensive, acquiring the food material is obviously not difficult. In nature, the mother frog feeds the tadpoles unfertilized eggs she produces and expels for this purpose.

Some tadpoles are born with large yolk reserves and will not begin taking outside foods for several days. It is a good idea not to feed new tadpoles for a day or two and to watch them carefully to see if they are eating the food when offered. If not, the uneaten food will foul their aquarium, so it should be strained out or otherwise removed with a net or aquarium vacuum cleaner.

It is important to feed tadpoles a variety of foods that are well endowed with the vitamins and minerals necessary for proper growth. Failure to do so will result in retarded growth, improper development, and an invariably fatal condition known as spindly leg syndrome seen in the newly metamorphosed froglets (see page 61 for more on this disease).

Chapter 6

Keeping Your Frog or Toad Healthy

Frogs do have medical problems, some of them quite serious and even fatal. Unfortunately, not many veterinarians and other experts on frogs and toads (collectively known as herpetologists) know enough about the diagnosis, care, and treatment of these animals' medical problems to establish a complete frog hospital—yet. However, considerable progress is being made in this area, thanks to the interest in these species from hobbyists, scientists, and environmentalists seeking a medical reason for the mysterious decline of frogs and toads in the wild.

The most common types of medical disorders among frogs and toads are infectious diseases—bacterial, viral, and fungal diseases. They also suffer from nutritional deficiencies, traumatic injuries, and a vague set of disorders best described as "constitutional" diseases. This last group of problems develops from improper housing, temperature, or diet, resulting in stress, compromised immunity, and failure to thrive. There is even a type of kidney cancer that is common in frogs, Lucke's renal adenocarcinoma, which is believed to be the result of such constitutional deficiencies.

Life Span in Captivity

The study of the natural life span of both captive and wild frogs and toads is an uncertain science about which very little is known. In the wild, it is difficult to mark young froglets and track them over time—although researchers are experimenting with a variety of electronic devices such as tiny subcutaneous tags or RFIDs (radio-frequency identification) that emit a radio signal on a particular frequency and can be pinpointed with a GPS device linked to a computer.

Captive frogs and toads can live for many years, and some species of bufo and the Argentinean horned frogs (*Ceratophrys sp.*) have been known to live fifteen to twenty years in captivity. One marine toad (*Bufo marinus*) is alleged to have lived thirty-five years in captivity and only died as a result of an unexpected accident, not natural causes. Even delicate, difficult to maintain, tiny species such as the dart-poison frogs have been known to reach the ripe old age of 15 years under ideal captive conditions. However, some species may live only a few years, and there are no clear and convincing records regarding the normal and expected life span of most frogs and toads.

One way to make sure your frog lives a long, healthy life is to keep its enclosure securely covered so it cannot escape.

One way to ensure the long life of your frogs and toads is to be sure they cannot escape from their housing. Captives that escape from their artificial environments are often doomed because of dehydration and lack of food; they are often are found dead and shriveled up days, weeks, or months after they went missing. Keeping your frog enclosure secure is essential to protect your frogs from this type of mishap.

Choosing a Veterinarian

It is best to pick out a veterinarian *before* you have a medical emergency. Finding a good veterinarian for your frog or toad may be one of your most difficult tasks. When considering prospective vets in your area, you should ask them if they have experience with amphibians. While most vets are well trained in small animal care, only a few have had any training in the unique medical requirements of amphibians.

The situation is improving though. The number of people with pet reptiles and amphibians has grown, and some veterinary practices now include the care of these animals in their exotics departments. You can find veterinarians who are qualified to work with amphibians by calling your local herpetological society or by searching online (see the appendix).

> ## Frog and Toad First-Aid Kit
>
> - Antiseptic solution (such as Betadine)
> - Antibiotic ointment (such as Neosporin or bacitracin)
> - Hydrogen peroxide
> - Very small pair of forceps (known as mosquito forceps or a mosquito clamp)
> - Small pair of blunt-tipped tweezers
> - Sterile, disposable, unpowdered gloves
> - 2×2 and 4×4 sterile gauze pads
> - Cotton-tipped swabs

If you cannot find a suitable veterinarian in your area, consider using a veterinarian nearby and having them call in consultations to a reptile and amphibian specialist.

The Best Way to Avoid Problems

The best way to avoid problems is to keep your frogs' habitat clean. Many species of frogs excrete toxins that do not pose a problem for them or their brethren in the wild, but that can build up rapidly in the closed environment of a captive habitat. It's yet another reason to keep their water extremely clean.

Frogs and toads are unusually susceptible to pesticide sprays and cleaning agents used in their immediate vicinity, so take great care to shield them from becoming poisoned by such agents. Never use detergents or household cleansers on frog, toad, or tadpole tanks. Empty an aquatic or semiaquatic frog's tank and rinse it only with hot tap water.

> **Cleaning Your Frog or Toad's Tank**
>
> At least once a day:
>
> Put on a pair of nonpowdered disposable plastic gloves.
>
> Remove all fecal wastes and bits of shed skin.
>
> Empty water bowls used for soaking and "ponds," rinse them in very hot chlorinated tap water, and refill with cool *dechlorinated* (aged) water.

The best way to avoid health problems is to keep your frog's habitat clean. Hot tap water is all you need to clean most surfaces.

Clean all water bowls, gravel, tank, and tank furnishings using nothing more than plain hot water, as well. Using any detergents may leave residue that will kill your frogs. Dry everything with fresh paper towels as traces of detergent left on cloth towels could bother your frogs. (You will also find specific care instructions for various species in chapter 7.)

Elaborate terrariums do not need to be frequently torn down and cleaned, and can go on for months, or even a year or more, if they are well planted. Use a paper towel dampened with water to clean the inside surface of the glass.

If it becomes necessary to use a disinfectant on your frog-related surfaces, a diluted solution of hydrogen peroxide is among the most innocuous and can be thoroughly rinsed away with hot water. Disinfectants such as Nolvasan, if recommended by your veterinarian, should be thoroughly rinsed away after they have been applied to any surfaces with which frogs or toads come in contact.

Infectious Microbial Diseases

Infectious or contagious diseases, also referred to as microbial diseases, can be caused by viruses, bacteria, fungi, and unicellular and multicellular parasites. Frogs and toads are susceptible to various types of all of these; however, some of these diseases are more prevalent than others.

Prevent harmful bacteria from multiplying by doing frequent water changes.

Red-Leg Disease

Perhaps the most common bacterial disease of frogs is red-leg disease. Red-leg disease causes the rear legs to become inflamed or reddened, and these bacteria ultimately attack the frog's blood and internal organs. At least two types of bacteria have been implicated as the cause of this condition: *Aeromonas hydrophila* and *Pseudomonas aeruginosa*.

The culprit bacteria are common in the environment, but in the wrong place under stressful and unhygienic conditions, they can become deadly. In humans, under similar circumstances, they can also result in pneumonia and other serious infections. Red-leg disease is extremely difficult to treat, and death is often inevitable. It can, however, be prevented by keeping your frogs under extremely clean conditions—which means daily or every other day water changes.

Although these bacteria can be treated with a number of common antibiotics, there is virtually no information as to the proper doses to use in frogs and toads and what the best route of administration would be. If the signs of red-leg are caught early enough, it may be worth trying tetracycline ointment externally over the infected areas. This is a prescription drug that your veterinarian must provide. You can also try an over-the-counter bacitracin ointment or a combination ointment containing both bacitracin and polymyxin-B.

Salmonella

Another common bacteria of frogs and toads is *Salmonella sp*. Because frogs and toads eat insects, and insects acquire *Salmonella* from the soil, it is not at all unusual to find this bacteria in the gastrointestinal tract of many frogs and toads. Kept in check by their immune systems, it is normal for them to carry this bacteria and it should not be treated—treatment could pose an unacceptable risk to the animal because so little is known about antibiotic dosages for frogs.

Frogs that become stressed, usually as a result of unfavorable captive conditions, become immunocompromised. Should this occur, the *Salmonella* bacteria could overproduce, resulting in severe diarrhea and dehydration leading to death. Once again, the best prevention is good care and habitat hygiene.

Fungal Diseases

Fungal diseases are rarer than would be expected in animals that live in moist, dark, damp environments. Most fungi attack open wounds, cuts, or abrasions in frogs. They appear as feathery or fluffy whitish or grayish masses of material. Any sign of these on a frog's body should be rapidly attended to in order to prevent fungal invasion. Once fungi attack internal structures or start traveling via the bloodstream, they become extremely difficult or impossible to treat.

Because fungal diseases are external, it may be possible to treat them externally with antifungal ointments, which you can get from your veterinarian. These diseases are also susceptible to externally applied tropical fish remedies, such as the dye malachite green—available at aquarium supply stores.

Viruses

Little is known of viruses that affect frogs, but there are a few pathogenic types specific to this group of animals. Scientists have even considered using the spread of frog-specific viruses as "weapons" in the fight against introduced species of frogs that are overrunning foreign habitats, such as the marine (or cane) toad in Australia; however, they were worried such agents might attack native species as well.

Parasites

Wild-caught frogs and toads can have a variety of internal single-cell and multi-cell parasites, such as tapeworms, nematodes, roundworms, and flukes, as well as a variety of amebas and similar protozoans. Internal parasite infections should be treated by a veterinarian, preferably one who is experienced with amphibians or who will access the information by networking with other informed veterinarians. Although there are known agents that will kill various internal parasites, little is known of their effect on frogs, the seriousness of their side effects on frogs, if any, or their proper dosages.

Occasionally, frogs and toads (particularly wild-caught ones) are found with external parasites, such as leeches, which can be picked off with a pair of tweezers. The resulting wound should be disinfected with Betadine ointment.

Wild-caught frogs may have a variety of internal parasites.

> ### Signs of a Poor Diet
>
> Among the signs of dietary or habitat deficiencies are excessive periods of time where your frog appears lighter or darker in color than usual, weak hind legs, a weak jaw, failure to eat, absence of defecation, inactivity or lethargy in a normally active species (some species normally sit still for long periods of time, such as the horned frogs), and the appearance of unusual skin secretions (don't touch them as they could be toxic). Faded colors in some species are an indication of a dietary deficiency that is best remedied by dusting feeder insects with a vitamin and mineral supplement.

Nutritional Disorders

Lack of a proper diet, or lack of a diet that closely resembles that of the wild frog or toad, can cause a number of serious afflictions. These include spindly leg syndrome and its relative, metabolic bone disease.

Metabolic Bone Disease

Frogs fed a diet that does not have enough calcium and phosphorus, particularly during development and growth periods, often suffer from metabolic bone disease. Among the more important nutrients needed to prevent this disorder is vitamin D_3. Several times a week, it is a good idea to dust crickets and other bugs with a supplement that contains this vitamin.

The earliest signs of metabolic bone disease in frogs and toads are difficulty in stalking, grabbing, and swallowing their food. Any frog that was able to do this before and suddenly seems to be having trouble trying to eat is probably starting to develop weaknesses in its bones and muscles, making it difficult for the frog to capture and eat food.

Whether or not frogs and toads need full-spectrum lighting to help them synthesize vitamin D_3 in their bodies, as some reptiles do, is still a matter of debate. However, it may prove worthwhile (mainly for daytime active, diurnal, species) to provide several hours of full-spectrum lighting over your frogs' enclosure. Species that remain in hiding during the day or that are active principally at night or during hours when there is naturally little sunlight probably would not benefit from full-spectrum lighting.

Some researchers believe full-spectrum lighting helps stimulate breeding in some species and, of course, it promotes plant growth if you have live plants in your terrarium or aqua-terrarium. On the other hand, excessive ultraviolet light has been blamed for killing some types of frog eggs and causing extinctions and near extinctions in the American Northwest, so it is

Dart-poison frogs are particularly susceptible to spindly leg syndrome, which is caused by nutritional deficiencies.

not recommended for developing eggs. The impact of artificial and excessive lighting is an area that has engendered much controversy, and it is not possible to make recommendations that would apply to all frogs.

Spindly Leg Syndrome

Dendrobatids, the dart-poison frogs, are particularly susceptible to spindly leg syndrome, which is seen in newly metamorphosed animals. It is believed that this illness is due to either nutritional deficiencies in the mother frog or in the food the froglet is fed (or quite possibly both). Therefore, it is best to dust insects fed to these frogs with a good vitamin-mineral supplement two or three times a week. These powdered preparations, which stick to bugs, can be purchased in most full-line pet supply stores. Be sure the supplement you buy contains calcium, phosphorus, and vitamin D_3 in addition to other trace elements and vitamins.

Intestinal Obstructions

Intestinal obstruction or fecal impaction usually occurs when frogs swallow gravel or sand along with their prey items. Occasionally, even a small, rounded piece of gravel can cause this condition. That's why you should definitely avoid placing food items on such substrates, which will stick to the prey and could cause intestinal problems in the frog.

Another cause of intestinal obstruction in some species is a steady diet of hard-shelled insects, such as beetles or their chitinous larvae (mealworms). Mealworms are a good food, but they should not be given to the exclusion of softer-bodied insects in the diet, such as crickets and waxworms.

Veterinary treatment, including surgical removal of the blockage, may be required. Before resorting to surgery, your veterinarian may try force-feeding a small dose of lubricating material, such as mineral oil, to see if this helps move the blockage though the animal's digestive system.

Chemical Intoxication

As previously mentioned, there are many substances in our environment that are dangerously toxic to frogs. These include soaps, detergents, surface disinfectants, pesticides, herbicides, fertilizers, paints, heavy metals, petroleum products, and many others. It is important to keep your frogs' enclosure as isolated as possible from these kinds of environmental contaminants.

Remember that a small amount of these substances can have a serious impact on your frogs' health, although the same amount would not bother you or your larger pets. Such materials may be, at least in part, responsible for the disappearance of frogs in the wild, and they are certain to kill your animals.

Traumatic Injuries

Cuts and abrasions in frogs and toads are best treated by applying Betadine ointment once or twice daily until healing or scarring is observed. External lesions can also be disinfected with sterile gauze soaked in hydrogen peroxide at the

Many substances that are common in our world can be extremely toxic to frogs.

strength sold in drug stores (3 percent dilution). Broken bones and major injuries that result in internal bleeding and loss of a limb, a foot, or a digit are often fatal. Frogs that do recover suffer from lifelong disabilities.

Handling Frogs and Toads

Frogs and toads should not be handled frequently or at all. They have delicate skin that is easy to injure, plus the soap residue and oils on human hands may harm them. However, circumstances will arise where it may be necessary to handle them. These might include examining them, treating cuts and bruises, moving them from their regular home to a holding tank while cleaning their main home, and taking them to the veterinarian or to a frog show.

The following is a short list of some of the tools you should have on hand in case it becomes necessary to handle your frogs or toads:

- At least two clean, fine-mesh, nylon fish nets. They should be large enough to accommodate your largest frog.
- A pair of clean, new (never used) plastic or wooden chopsticks.
- An 8-inch length of clear plastic tubing 1 inch in diameter. This can be purchased in most aquarium supply shops. Also find two corks or caps that fit snugly on the end of this tubing. You will need this tubing if you keep and need to handle tiny frogs less than 1 inch long.
- Clear, clean plastic food storage dishes with predrilled air holes that can be used as temporary holding containers or transport boxes for your frogs. You can also use a clean plastic bucket (one that was never used to hold soaps or detergents) fitted with a snug lid of screening or netting.
- A box of disposable surgical gloves. These must be unpowdered. If you're sensitive to latex, there are some that are latex-free. Such gloves come in small, medium, and large. Use gloves whenever you're handling the frogs and when you're doing dirty cleaning chores associated with your frogs. After you're finished, dispose of the gloves properly and wash your hands with soap and hot water.

Before handling any frog, be sure to wash your hands and rinse them thoroughly to remove all traces of soap. Put on a clean pair of disposable gloves, if at all possible. Frogs larger than 1 inch in length should

> **TIP**
>
> If it is necessary to transport your frog, place its carrying case in a thermo-insulated Styrofoam cooler to protect against temperature extremes.

Pick up your frog by scooping it up in a fish net. Be sure to support it underneath and cover it on top to prevent escape.

be scooped up in one fish net and quickly covered over with a second net to prevent them from leaping out of the net. They can then be coaxed into a smaller holding container while you work on their regular quarters or transport them.

Tiny Frogs

Very tiny frogs, such as the dart-poison frogs and other small species, should never be picked up. It is too easy to harm such small, delicate creatures by holding them in your hands. This is where the 1-inch diameter clear plastic tubing comes in. With one end corked, place the open end near the frog and gently coax it to hop into the tube with a chopstick. When it is well inside the tube, quickly cap the entrance end.

You can now examine the froglet at close range, even using a magnifying glass to see tiny structures, without ever touching it. The tube trick can also be used to transport these tiny frogs from one container to the next. If you intend to keep the frog in the tube for five minutes or more, make sure that you have punched a few small air holes in the plastic beforehand.

Holding Larger Frogs

If it is necessary to hold larger species, the best way is to grasp them around the waist, restraining their rear legs in a straight and downward position. Even then, some frogs are quite slippery and will try to get away from you—and some will succeed. It takes a certain amount of practice to know exactly how much force to exert. Too much can obviously harm the frog and too little can permit it to escape.

Most frogs and toads do not like being held. The thought, if any, that must be racing through their minds is that they are going to be eaten at any moment. This causes them to be less than ceremonious in your presence, and they will urinate or even defecate on you in a bid for you to drop your attention and give them a moment to escape. Do not be startled by this, and stand your ground regardless of the insults your frog or toad may heap upon you.

Some frogs, on the other hand, are quite placid and still, and will gladly perch on your open hand for prolonged periods without worrying about their safety. Tree frogs, in particular, are fond of attaching themselves to one's hand or arm, as it gives them a perch well above ground level, and this is their favorite vantage point.

Froggy Dangers to People

Frogs are about the most innocuous and innocent members of the animal kingdom and serve overwhelmingly to help, not hurt, human beings. Nonetheless, some frog species are dangerously poisonous—capable of secreting toxins that are characterized as among the most poisonous substances on earth. Every incident of one of these toxins poisoning or killing a human has been related to foolish and risky behavior by the human, not the frog!

This marine toad is oozing toxin from the paratoid gland.

In one recent spate of cases in New York City, a number of young men swallowed a Chinese drug known as Shen Su, which was supposed to be applied externally. It contained dangerous *bufotoxins,* or toad poisons, and several men died and others were hospitalized in critical condition. Fraternity pranksters on occasion make pledges swallow goldfish, but when toad licking was substituted there were near deadly consequences.

Serious hobbyists, aware of the dangerous secretions of some species, have never been harmed by their frogs, thanks to careful precautions. Under no circumstances should a tadpole, frog, or toad be placed in the mouth or swallowed. Yes, many cultures eat frogs. But frogs' legs are thoroughly cleaned and the skin is removed before they are cooked. Even then, only certain species of frogs' legs are safe to eat, and on occasion improperly cooked legs have caused parasite infections in the people who ate them.

Do They Bite?

Although 99 percent of the more than 5,200 different kinds of frogs in the world do not bite humans, there are a few species with sharp, frontally situated teeth that could give an unwary handler a nasty cut (and that would be the worst of it). These species include the popular horned frogs (also known as Pac-Man frogs) and the African bullfrog (*Pyxiecephalus sp.*).

Make sure that all frog bites that break the skin are thoroughly disinfected, and seek medical attention quickly if they become swollen, inflamed, painful, or

This Chaco horned frog is one of the few species that bite.

tender. No frog can deliver poison via its bite, but there may be harmful bacteria present in the frog's mouth that could be introduced into the bloodstream by a bite wound.

As a matter of first aid, all animal bites should be thoroughly washed in soap and hot water and then disinfected by soaking in a basin of Betadine solution for an hour or more. If this is not possible, quickly wash the bitten area and at least apply the disinfectant and dress the bite with a sterile bandage.

Sharing Bacteria

Rarely will a pet frog develop a form of cutaneous tuberculosis known as *Mycobacterium marinum.* This disease causes large granulomatous lesions on the skin and is contagious to humans. If a frog has any strange-looking skin lesions or bumps, be sure not to touch it with bare hands and to seek veterinary attention quickly. If you have touched the lesion, check with your doctor, who can determine if you have become infected.

The condition is easy to treat and is not fatal. Fishermen get it from handling infected fish, and even swimmers get it from swimming in contaminated swimming pools. In fact, for this reason it is sometimes called *swimming pool granuloma.*

Frogs may also harbor *Salmonella, E. coli, Pseudomonas* and *Aeromonas* bacteria, as well as a variety of protozoan and fungal microorganisms that can also infect humans. However, because frogs and toads really should be handled cautiously and infrequently, such diseases are rarely a problem for humans. Those at most risk are children under 8 years of age, pregnant women, and people who are immunocompromised for any reason. Such people should avoid contact with animals such as frogs and toads. In households that include high-risk people and frogs, caretakers of the frogs should be diligent in washing thoroughly after handling the frogs or doing frog-related chores, such as cleaning out water bowls or dropping in food. Direct contact with the animal is not necessary for someone at risk to be infected. Bacteria are most commonly carried on the hands of the person in contact with the frog, who passes them to the next person by touch or through touching food and eating utensils.

> Infectious diseases that are transmittable from animals to humans, and vice versa, are called *zoonotic diseases.*

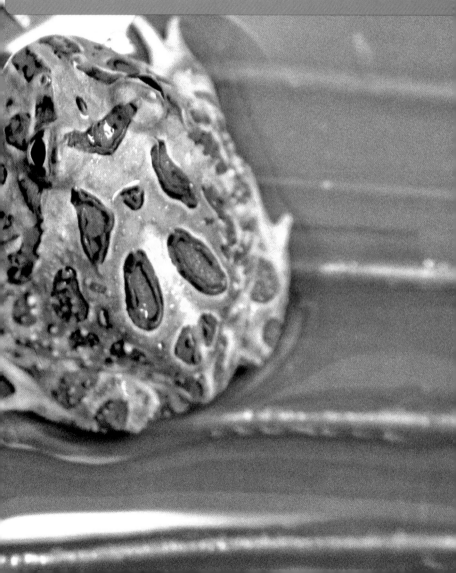

Part III

Frogs and Toads in Our World

Chapter 7

The Variety of Frogs and Toads

T he world of frogs and toads contains some forty-one families, hundreds of genera, and thousands of species. Only those groups that commonly find their way into the hobbyist trade and are the most popular and/or most commonly available species will be discussed here.

Due to recent revisions in the names of the frog and toad families, and with further changes being debated all the time, each family is being identified here only by its simple English name. Neither hobbyists nor the frogs and toads they keep have much of a need to know the technical scientific family names they go by. Of course, this subject is of great importance to specialists engaged in the taxonomy (classification) and nomenclature of these animals, and is a field that advanced hobbyists might decide later to study. Genus and species names, as well as the most commonly accepted nonscientific names, are used in this chapter to identify each animal.

Frogs are typically measured from the tip of the snout to the cloacal vent. This a standardized measure is known as snout-vent length or s-v length.

Disc or Flat-Tongued Frogs

All members of this family are commonly seen in the hobby, and a number of species are bred in captivity. They include the painted frogs (*Discoglossus sp.*), the midwife toads (*Alytes sp.*), and the fire-bellied toads (*Bombina sp.*). The Oriental fire-bellied toad (*Bombina orientalis*) is the most common and popular member of the family. Painted frogs and midwife toads also show up in the pet trade.

Painted Frogs

The painted frog (*Discoglossus pictus*) and some five other species of this genus are found in Portugal, Spain, Israel, and on Corsica and Sardinia. Few members of this family, other than the painted frog, are readily available in the United States. The Israeli species, *Discoglossus nigriventer,* or black-bellied painted frog, is near extinction.

This species has a variety of colors and patterns and, despite its name, might appear rather drab by comparison to other species. Painted frogs require an extremely large enclosure and eat a variety of small insects, including crickets, chopped earthworms, and aphids.

Midwife Toads

There are three species of the genus *Alytes,* the midwife toads. The olive midwife toad (*Alytes obstetricians*) and the other two members of this genus, the brown midwife toad (*Alytes cisternasii*) and the Majorca midwife toad (*Alytes muletensis*), are best known for the active role the father plays in caring for a mated pair's eggs. The olive midwife toad is found in Great Britain and elsewhere in western Europe, the brown variety in Portugal, and, of course, the Majorca midwife toad is from the Spanish island of Majorca. This island species was discovered in 1979—due, no doubt, to the fact that it is found in fairly remote, mountainous habitats.

Olive Midwife Toad

The olive midwife toad is a small species and requires small- to medium-size insect fare and a large terrarium with a removable pool or pond in the form of a sunken plastic dish (clean and refill daily). This toad prefers cool, damp conditions with temperatures ranging from 65 degrees to 75 degrees Fahrenheit. Free-ranging outdoor breeding colonies of these unique toads have been established in several locations in Great Britain. Numerous attempts have been made to breed this species in captivity; so far, they have failed to produce any results.

Fire-Bellied Toads

Six species of the genus *Bombina* are known, ranging from western Europe to Turkey, Ukraine, eastern Asia, Russia, China, Korea, and Vietnam. Commonly referred to as the fire-bellied toads because of their colorful underbellies, some species are more colorful and popular than others. One species has a yellow underbelly and has interbred with other fire-bellied forms to produce an orange-bellied hybrid in the Danube Valley in Austria.

Fire-bellied toads can endure a wide range of temperatures, from 65 to 80 degrees Fahrenheit. They are a relatively small species, reaching 2½ to 3 inches in s-v length, and should be housed only with similar-size members of their own species. Similar frogs will try to swallow the arms and legs of tankmates when food is crawling nearby!

Fire-bellied toads should not be mixed with other species because they secrete a toxin called bombesin that could harm or even kill other species. In fact, their secretions can build up in tank water and possibly harm themselves, which is why their semiaquatic habitat should include a powerful carbon filter; even with filtration, 50 percent water changes at least every two days and complete water changes at least once a week are vital.

Fire-bellied toads are voracious eaters and will even attempt to eat smaller members of their own species. They will eat a wide variety of insect matter, including earthworms, mealworms, crickets, and fruit flies. Larger earthworms should be chopped into smaller pieces—they will continue to wriggle and attract the attention of the frogs.

These are attractive, easy to keep, lively little frogs. They are best housed in a filtered aquarium (at least ten gallons, and larger is better) landscaped with rock formations jutting just above or near the surface so they can climb out on them. You'll need a screen cover to keep the frogs in the tank.

Bombina toads are active both day and night and can often be seen basking in the sunlight—a very rare behavior for frogs but quite common in reptiles. A low-wattage incandescent or full-spectrum fluorescent lighting fixture can be turned on for several hours a day. If you do use a light, make sure it does not give off too much heat because these toads don't like the added warmth.

Fire-bellied toads are voracious eaters but are otherwise easy to keep.

These toads are readily available, and many hobbyists and professionals are captive-breeding them both for the pet trade and for medical research, because their skin secretions have important medical applications and are even being investigated for the treatment of gastrointestinal problems and some kinds of cancers in humans.

If you're lucky, you will hear them call. Their voice is highly unusual and delightful to hear.

Yellowbelly Toad

The yellowbelly toad (*Bombina variegata*) is a native of Europe. It has a greenish back and a yellow underbelly interspersed with blotches of black. This species grows to about 1½ inches, s-v length.

The yellowbelly toad (on top) and the European fire-bellied toad (below) can be quite messy.

They can be fed any insect small enough for them to swallow. You may try to feed them some live tropical fish foods, such as tubifex or white worms, if available; if not, half-grown crickets, fruit flies, and small mealworms are a good choice. Like all frogs, they should be fed at least once a day.

These little frogs foul their tank water rapidly, even with an excellent filtration system, so several times a week about half the water should be siphoned off and replaced. About every ten days it is necessary to do a complete water change and to clean out the filter system.

European Fire-Bellied Toad

The European fire-bellied toad (*Bombina bombina*) is found in northern Europe. This is also a small species and resembles the yellowbelly, except that its belly is orange or red with some black. Care is basically the same.

Oriental Fire-bellied Toad

The Oriental fire-bellied toad (*Bombina orientalis*) is found throughout northeastern Asia. Wild-caught specimens are exported in great numbers from China and appear regularly in the pet trade. However, local captive-born animals are the best choice when obtaining these beautiful little toads. They are bright green and black above, and their bellies have a bright red and black pattern. They reach an s-v length of about 2 inches and should have plenty of space—two adults should

Make sure you get a captive-bred Oriental fire-bellied toad.

have at least a ten-gallon aquarium to live in, and larger groups need correspondingly larger aquariums.

They can be fed a variety of insects that should be dusted with a good vitamin-mineral supplement containing carotene, which this frog needs to maintain its beautiful red coloration. Most captive-reared insects are apt to be raised on bland meals that do not contain this essential element. You could also try feeding food insects carrots or other yellow veggies to gut-load them with carotene before feeding them to the toads.

Giant Yunnan Fire-bellied Toad

The giant Yunnan fire-bellied toad (*Bombina maxima*), that is slightly larger than the Oriental fire-bellied toad, is occasionally available in the pet trade. It prefers deeper waters to swim around in (8 to 10 inches deep), and so needs a larger aquarium. These toads also require rafts or rock formations in their housing so that they can come out of the water to eat and bask in the light. This species prefers cooler temperatures (in nature, it ranges from southern China to eastern Siberia), and will remain active at temperatures as low as 50 degrees Fahrenheit.

Giant Yunnan fire-bellied toads will eat larger insects, such as half-grown to three-quarter-grown crickets, mealworms, and flies. Gut-loading such bugs carotene or dusting the bugs with a good vitamin supplement helps these toads to maintain their vivid red underbelly.

There are several other species of fire-bellied toads from inside China, but these are never exported to the United States. These include the Hubei and the Guangxi fire-bellied toads.

Tailed Frogs

This family of frogs contains just two living genera—the tailed frog (*Ascaphus truei*) of the northwestern United States and southwestern Canada, which are occasionally available, and three other species of the genus *Leiopelma,* which are confined to New Zealand and are never seen in the pet or hobbyist trade.

The so-called tail, seen only on males, is really an *intromittant* organ, used to practice an internal method of fertilization. The tailed frog is the only species of frog that engages in true sexual intercourse, although the three species from New Zealand also engage in internal fertilization of ova but do so by cloacal contact—very much like the method birds use to fertilize eggs.

Tailed frogs are small species, reaching s-v lengths of less than 1 inch. The tailed frog is primarily an aquatic species and should be kept in an aqua-terrarium at relatively cool temperatures ranging from 65 degrees to 75 degrees Fahrenheit. They can be fed small crickets, tubifex worms, and aquatic insect larvae.

True Toads

This is a huge family with more than 20 genera and more than 300 living species. The largest group are the toads in the genus *Bufo,* with more than 200 species. Also referred to as bufonid toads, they are found throughout the world. They live mainly on land, going to water only to breed and occasionally to take in water by absorption through their dorsal surfaces. One bufonid, the Malayan climbing toad, is found in low-lying brush and trees.

Many of the true toads are excellent starter species. Primarily terrestrial in nature, these toads can be kept either in elaborate terrariums with water dishes large enough to

Very large members of the Bufo family include the marine toad.

accommodate them (clean once or twice daily), or in simple aquariums with paper towels as substrate and a water dish. If you get lucky and find a Malayan climbing toad, a few branches to climb will make it feel right at home.

Although these toads come from a large number of different climatic conditions, virtually all can be successfully kept in the 70- to 80-degree Fahrenheit range. They generally abhor great heat, and in the wild can often be found dug into the moist substrate in the shade during the hottest part of the day. They are most active at cooler times, such as at dawn, dusk, and night, and can often be found around suburban homes with insect-attracting lights. The toads lie in wait in the shadows to feast on the bugs drawn to such lights as they fall to the ground.

What to feed a bufo toad depends mainly on the toad's size. Large bufo toads can eat small mice without a problem. Some large toads have been observed gobbling up dog food left outside houses in bowls for yard dogs. It is not, therefore, a good idea to leave dog food outside in areas populated by bufo toads, because the dog, as often as not, comes along and bites the toad, releasing glandular poisons into the dog's mouth. If swallowed, the poison could kill the dog. Moreover, dog food is not designed for toads and could cause dietary imbalances that will adversely affect the toad's health. (The principal glands containing toxic substances are located above the toad's shoulders to the rear of the eyes, and contain a digitalis-like poison.)

Smaller species of toads will also eat all kinds of insects, including crickets, mealworms, moths, flies, beetles, and spiders—virtually anything they can swallow, including other frogs, lizards, and even small snakes.

Large toads, in the 6- to 8-inch s-v range, include the marine toad (known as the cane toad in Australia) (*Bufo marinus*), the Blomberg's toad (*Bufo blombergi*), and the Colorado River toad (*Bufo alvarius*). The Colorado River toad is becoming very scarce throughout most of its range, and it is becoming increasingly difficult to find these animals as pets, although a few are still available on occasion. This is a large toad that is definitely worth breeding because of its increasing scarcity and its pretty markings (making it popular as a pet): slate gray, glossy rhinolike skin with orange spots. It is a legally protected species in some areas.

The Colorado River toad is becoming scarce in its natural habitat.

Common American (*Bufo americanus*) and southern (*Bufo terrestris*) toads, and other small to medium species in the 2- to 5-inch s-v range, can be fed crickets, mealworms on occasion (not as a steady diet), earthworms, moths, flies, and beetles. Such toads are still very populous in many locations, and you can try your hand at collecting a few yourself (check local game laws first). They are very plentiful and are not a protected species in most areas. They are a great starter species and cost either nothing or very little if you buy them.

The harlequin frogs (*Atelopus sp.*) are found in South and Central America. They are beautiful, colorful toads with poisonous skin secretions. These species are becoming increasingly scarce and are subject to international protection. They do not thrive in captivity, although the few keepers who have managed to obtain these toads have found that they are voracious eaters of small insects; like well-planted, well-ventilated cages; and prefer temperatures in the mid-70s Fahrenheit.

Endangered Toads

There are five domestic toads on the United States endangered species list: the Houston toad (*Bufo houstonensis*), the Puerto Rican crested toad (*Peltophryne lemur*), the Wyoming toad (*Bufo baxteri*), the southwestern arroyo toad (*Bufo microscaphus*), and the Sonoran green toad (*Bufo retiformis*). The United States also protects an additional seventeen frog and toad species, many of them from overseas, and the CITES list (see page 120 for more on CITES) is larger still. But with all the thousands of different frogs and toads, it still leaves a very large selection for hobbyists to keep and study.

Popular American Bufo Toads

We present here a few of the most popular and widely available North American species of bufonid toads that are suitable as pets. Most of these toads are not endangered in most locations. In fact, after transforming from tadpoles to toadlets they migrate across roads to reach other bodies of water and often are killed by auto traffic, which cannot avoid them because they are so plentiful.

American Toad

The American toad (*Bufo americanus*) is the most common toad of the eastern United States, ranging from the tip of New England to northern Georgia, and across the Midwest from Minnesota to Mississippi. It is also found throughout central and northeastern Canada.

This species prefers cool, moist habitats and is active principally at night, on cool, overcast days, and at dusk and dawn. It eats virtually any kind of bug it can find and is a voracious eater. In fact, it is reliably estimated that a single adult American toad swallows up to 100 insects a day, 3,000 a month, and nearly 10,000 over the course of a single summer season.

The American toad has few natural enemies, but the family of hognose snakes (*Heterodon sp.*) a mildly venomous type of snake also known as rear-fanged snakes, specializes in eating such toads and is not deterred by the toad's poisonous glandular secretions. Other toad predators, such as crows, have learned to flip them on their backs and eat them from the belly, studiously avoiding the poison glands on their dorsal surfaces.

A single adult or pair of American toads can be housed comfortably in a ten- to fifteen-gallon terrarium with a water dish and plain paper toweling substrate or a bottom layer of pebbles with sterile potting soil on top. A water dish large enough to accommodate all the members of the toad tank should be provided, and emptied and refilled at least once a day. This enables them to soak themselves and absorb water through their skin—which is customary for all amphibians.

Southern Toad

The southern toad (*Bufo terrestris*) is found throughout the southeastern United States, from coastal Virginia through Florida and westward to Louisiana.

These southern toads are mating.

Southern toads are at home in sandy areas, remain burrowed just beneath the surface, and come out at night to forage or to mate. Like American toads, they will eat virtually any animated insect prey.

If kept in a landscaped terrarium, a sandy loam or potting soil substrate is best. A water dish to one side should be provided for the toad to soak; this must be emptied and refilled daily.

Fowler's Toad and Woodhouse's Toad

The Fowler's toad (*Bufo woodhousi fowleri*) is a subspecies of the Woodhouse's toad and is found throughout the eastern half of the United States westward to the Mississippi. The subspecies is named after early Massachusetts field biologist S.P. Fowler.

The primary species, a more western ranging species, *Bufo woodhousei*, is named in honor of the early southwestern surgeon and explorer Samuel Washington Woodhouse. Their care and housing requirements are the same as those for the American toad.

Red Spotted Toad

The red spotted toad (*Bufo punctatus*) is found in the arid southwestern United States and shares its habitat with the spadefoot toad. It is a small (about 3 inches maximum s-v length), pretty species dotted with red spots against a slate gray

The Woodhouse's toad tends to be active when the sun goes down.

background. A terrarium carpeted with sandy soil and a mix of stones or rocks is ideal for this species. It prefers temperatures in the 70- to 80-degree Fahrenheit range. Like other Bufo toads, it will eat a wide variety of lively, animated insect prey of suitable size.

Popular Imported Bufo Toads

Europe and Asia also have their share of bufo toads, some of which are occasionally imported into the United States. The European common toad (*Bufo bufo*) is found throughout northern Europe and reaches about 6 inches in s-v length. The natterjack toad (*Bufo calamita*) is a smaller species, about 4 inches in s-v length. The pretty green toad (*Bufo virdis*) reaches about 5 inches in s-v length. Care for these three common European species is virtually the same. They require sandy soil or a plain paper towel substrate, a water dish, and a terrarium of adequate size (about one gallon per inch of toad). They relish slugs, earthworms, and most insects small enough to swallow whole.

The natterjack toad is protected in most of its range throughout Europe as the frog is classified as a declining species in many areas where it was once plentiful.

The Java toad (*Bufo asper*) and the black-spined toad (*Bufo melanosticus*) are two common bufonids available from Asia. Both species prefer temperatures in the 70s Fahrenheit. The Java toad is the largest Asian bufo, reaching s-v lengths of approximately 8 inches.

The European common toad likes to swallow insects whole.

Dart-Poison Frogs

The arrow or dart-poison frogs, collectively known as dendrobatids, are so named because certain native groups in South America use the deadly skin secretions of these frogs to tip their hunting arrows or blow-gun darts. Despite the fact that some of these species generate extremely toxic poisons and a few species generate sufficient amounts to kill hundreds of adult humans, not one hobbyist has ever been poisoned by one of these frogs.

The bright colors of poison frogs are warning signals to predators that they harbor toxins. Some of the less brilliantly colored dendrobatids do not seem to be as poisonous as their brightly colored relatives, and a group of them, the dull-colored rocket frogs (*Colostethus sp.*), are probably only mildly poisonous.

There are a growing number of dart-poison frog enthusiasts throughout the world, including many Americans. The amazing popularity of these frogs is due to their mystique and also to their unbelievably beautiful colors and patterns. The fact that many of their toxic secretions are also being explored for their medical uses makes them no less interesting. And finally, the amazing degree of parental care they give their offspring makes it hard to believe these animals are mere amphibians, rather than birds or mammals.

Dart-poison frogs are expensive—$25 to more than $150—so it is strongly advised that before you invest money, time, and energy in these animals, you learn as much as you can about them. See the appendix for additional resources on the care of these frogs, and read all back issues of the many dart-poison frog newsletters out there. The more informed you are, the better off you will be. Armed with a thorough knowledge of these frogs, you might then consider buying one or a pair of a captive-bred species to get your feet wet.

*The golden poison frogs (*Phyllobates*) are the most toxic members of the family, and should never be handled barehanded.*

Dendrobatids are naturally found only in Central and South America. One species, the green and black dart-poison frog (*Dendrobates auratus*), was introduced into the upper Manoa Valley of Oahu, Hawaii, in 1932 to control mosquitoes. The descendants of the original 206 specimens, collected from small islands off the Pacific coast of Panama, still survive today in isolated populations in the moist valleys of Oahu. Studies of their poisonous skin toxins reveal that they differ markedly from the toxins secreted by their forebears back in Panama, lending further credence to the theory that their poisons are somehow linked to their native diet.

Dendrobatids are excellent climbers, so they need to be secured in well-covered, screened-over terrariums. They are best housed singly or in pairs, as their skin secretions can poison themselves and other species in the same container. They do best if provided with live plants—bromeliads or *epiphytes* (air plants).

Although they are primarily arboreal, they also need moisture. A shallow water dish that they can easily climb in and out of (use small, smooth stones as stepping blocks, if necessary) should be provided. Change the water at least once a day to prevent the buildup of both waste matter and poisonous skin secretions. Be sure to flush the old water down the toilet; do not throw it anywhere where its poisons may harm plants and animals. Take care not to spill or splash it around. Use disposable rubber gloves for this chore. Replace the water with fresh, aged (dechlorinated) water after rinsing the dish, preferably with a good flushing of water from an outside hose—with the run-off directed into a sewer drain.

*Supposedly, the poison from the skin of the phantasmal poison frog (*Epipedobates*) contains a potent painkiller.*

Poison Frogs as Pets

Probably the most popular poison frog pets are *Dendrobates,* the dart-poison frogs. This genus contains about thirty dazzlingly colorful but poisonous species. Hobbyists have been unharmed by these frogs for several reasons. First, the import of all dendrobatid frogs is regulated, and many are strictly protected by international treaties. All dendrobatid frogs appear on the U.S. endangered species list and most are listed with CITES, limiting their importation. (See page 120 for an explanation of what a CITES listing means.) As a result, most of the frogs in the pet trade are captive-bred, and captive-bred frogs do not seem to have as deadly a group of poisons as their wild counterparts. This is undoubtedly related to their diet in the wild. Captive frogs are not fed the same insects that they would eat in their native forests, and the insects they are fed do not eat the same poisonous plants as the insects eaten by wild frogs. This is an example of how a deadly toxin works its way up the food chain. Insects eat poisonous plants and have miniscule amounts of these plant poisons in their bodies. The frogs eat thousands of these insects, obtaining the raw materials to synthesize far greater and far stronger toxins than even the insects or their plant food have. The frogs have been jokingly referred to as "mobile chemical factories."

In contrast, captive-bred and long-term wild-caught captives are fed innocuous insects that do not eat toxic plants, thus the frog, if it ever had a deadly skin toxin, soon loses the ability to make more of it. Obviously this is good news for hobbyists who worry about such things. Notably, however, not all frogs and not all toxins present in frogs are related to conditions in the wild. There are still plenty of captive-bred frogs and toads that are just as toxic as their cousins in the wild, so do not become complacent in handling these animals or allowing children or pets access to them. You can never really know unless you have a state-of-the-art biochemistry lab at your disposal.

So what about frogs that are still very poisonous or frogs that were held by hobbyists and breeders before captive-breds became widely available? The answer lies in careful handling. Handling such frogs with bare hands can be detrimental to the frogs as well as to the handler. See the discussion of handling in chapter 6 for tips on how to work with these little poisonous frogs so both you and the frog are suitably protected.

Feeding dart-poison frogs is somewhat problematic. They are voracious eaters and, given a steady supply of the right size bugs, they will eat incessantly during daylight. Providing a steady supply of small enough bugs is one of the most difficult challenges a dart-poison frog keeper faces. It is estimated that a single adult dart-poison frog could easily consume about 100 ants or fruit flies a day, which means that anyone thinking about keeping these frogs should seriously think about establishing ant and wingless fruit fly colonies, as well. They will also eat pinhead-size crickets, which can be commercially purchased by mail order. (A list of suppliers of live insect foods is included in the appendix.) Alternative food choices include termites, aphids, small fly larvae, and other small bugs.

Experts advise that your frogs are certain to die after just two to three days without food, so it is critical that you have plenty of food on hand at all times. Going on vacation is also a problem, unless you have someone reliable to take over the feeding and cleaning. This is why most pet shops do not like to stock these frogs.

One alternative is to take your frogs and their food supply with you in small traveling plastic terrariums, which are available in pet shops. Obviously, there has to be a lot of strategic planning involved in such an effort. Some hosts may prefer that you leave your frogs and their bugs at home. Your only other option is to take a lot of day trips and when you get home at midnight, rush in to feed your frogs and clean out their water bowl before you do anything else. Do the same thing early in the morning before you depart. Otherwise, you will have to find a reliable "frog sitter" to do these chores while you are away.

Dendrobatids are particularly susceptible to a disease called spindly leg syndrome. See chapter 6 for information on this nutritional disorder.

Because the dendrobatids are diurnal, tropical species, it is safe to assume that they prefer light and warmth (75 to 85 degrees Fahrenheit) during the day, cooler temperatures at night (70 to 75 degrees Fahrenheit), and high humidity at all times. If you

> **T I P**
>
> **The Right Name**
>
> The dart-poison frogs are often mislabeled poison dart frogs. The incorrect name implies that the frogs are darts themselves, when in fact, they only supply the poison for the dart. The early literature on these frogs was in foreign languages, where the terms were correctly reversed due to the semantic rules of those languages. Unfortunately, the terms were then incorrectly translated.

set up a large terrarium for these frogs, use a secure screen cover and manually mist it several times a day. If you do not have time to mist, you may want to buy or build a timer-controlled rainmaking system (see chapter 4). By planting your terrarium well, you also help to maintain humidity. Droplets of water on leaves enable the frogs to absorb needed moisture through their skin. (Frogs and toads do not drink water.) Use artificial full-spectrum light and avoid direct sunlight and heat-emitting incandescent bulbs, which can overheat the terrarium. If necessary, external sources of heat can be provided using undertank heating pads controlled either by thermostats or manually with the judicious use of a thermometer.

Popular Dart-Poison Frogs

These animals include the members of the genus *Dendrobates*.

Green and Black Dart-Poison Frog

This species is native to Costa Rica and ranges from Panama to western Colombia, and has been introduced onto Oahu, Hawaii. The green and black dart-poison frog (*Dendrobates auratus*) is widely available from captive-bred

stock and was the first and easiest of these frogs to breed in captivity. They grow to a maximum of 2½ inches s-v length.

These frogs require a well-planted terrarium with a water bowl, hiding places, and branches. The terrarium should have a secure cover. They eat a variety of small insects and are recommended for beginning dart-poison frog hobbyists.

The green and black dart-poison frog is the easiest to breed in captivity.

The blue dart-poison frog is very rare in the frog world.

Blue Dart-Poison Frog

The blue or azure dart-poison frog (*Dendrobates azureus*) is extremely beautiful and a great rarity because of its blue color—a color that is not common among frogs. The species was first discovered in 1969 in Surinam on the northern coast of South America. It reaches about 1½ inches s-v length, eats small insects, and is housed in the same fashion as all other dendrobatids. These frogs are being increasingly bred in captivity.

Red and Black Dart-Poison Frog

The red and black, or harlequin, dart-poison frog (*Dendrobates histrionicus*) averages about 1½ inches s-v length and is native to western Colombia and Ecuador. This species displays an amazing variety of patterns and color varieties. Some are black and yellow, some are black and red, and yet others are orange and black. These frogs are best avoided by beginning dart-poison frog hobbyists, as they are difficult to maintain in captivity.

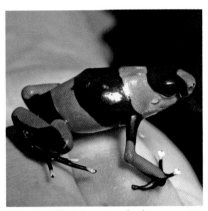

The red and black dart-poison frog has an amazing array of pattern and color variations.

Yellow-Banded Dart-Poison Frog

This species (*Dendrobates leucomelas*) is a somewhat heavier and more robust member of the group, growing to about 1½ inches s-v length. The yellow-banded dart-poison frog ranges from Guyana to Venezuela. It has bright yellow bands crowning the top of the head, extending vertically down the sides of the back on a jet black background. This frog will eat larger prey than most dart-poison frogs, and thus may be easier to feed. Its hearty constitution makes the yellow-banded dart-poison frog a good choice for beginners.

The yellow-banded dart-poison frog is one of the biggest members of the group.

Strawberry Dart-Poison Frog

The strawberry dart-poison frog (*Dendrobates pumilio*) is a bright metallic red frog with black or mottled black and gray legs. It is native to Costa Rica and Panama. This is a

The strawberry dart-poison frog needs a steady diet of extremely small insects.

small species, reaching about 1 inch s-v length. It requires a steady diet of extremely small live insects, such as aphids, ants, and pinhead crickets. This is a difficult species to rear in captivity and is not recommended for beginners.

The dyeing dart-poison frog is bigger and can eat bigger bugs.

Dyeing Dart-Poison Frog

This species (*Dendrobates tinctorius*) is among the largest of this genus of frogs, reaching nearly 2½ inches s-v length. In the wild, this frog lives in the Guyanas. This species has a number of highly variable color and pattern varieties, mainly in the blacks, grayish-blues, and yellows. Because of its size when full grown, it will eat larger prey items such as half-grown crickets, small moths, and other small to medium insects.

Glass Frogs

The frogs in this family have translucent skin. When viewed with a bright light behind them, you can see skeletal structures and other anatomical structures very much as if you were looking at an X-ray. There are three genera of glass frogs: *Centrolenella, Cochranella,* and *Hyalinobatrachium,* with approximately eighty-five species. This is a group in which new species are being discovered regularly. They are rarely available in the pet trade, as they fare poorly in captivity and do not ship very well.

Glass frogs need a well-planted terrarium with a substrate of damp, sandy soil, a water dish, and a steady supply of small insects. Most species are small, ranging in size from ¾ of an inch to 3 inches s-v length, depending on the species. Many are green, lime green, yellow, or yellowish green. They are a slim, active species that need to be fed daily and prefer temperatures in the high 60s to low 70s Fahrenheit, as they are found in cool, mountainous regions.

If you are lucky enough to get one of these oddities, take good care of it. It's likely to be the Fleischmann's glass frog (*Centrolenella fleischmanni*), which has a wide range extending from southern Mexico throughout Central America and over all of northern South America. A small, noncontiguous population also exists in parts of northern Argentina and southern Brazil.

You can see right through the glass frog's skin.

Tree Frogs

The tree frogs are a large group, with more than seventy-five species and even more subspecies—and new types are being discovered and described virtually every month. This is among the most worldwide and cosmopolitan of the frog families, with representatives found throughout North, Central, and most of South America. Members of the family also can be found in Australia, New Guinea, Tasmania, and the Solomon Islands, as well as throughout most of western Asia, China, Japan, and coastal North Africa. They are present on many tropical islands, too, often stowing away on ships to reach these locations.

Not all tree frogs live in trees. Some inhabit low-lying shrubs and some even spend time on the ground, although this is not true of most tree frogs. Many tree frogs do well around human dwellings and have no problem finding a home perched on walls, roof eaves, window ledges, doorway overhangs, drainpipes, and other building structures. Tree frogs that live on the outside of houses soon learn about nightlights and the bugs they attract. So while toads remain on the ground to catch bugs that drop to earth, tree frogs creep along the walls, in the shadows near the lights, waiting to feed upon the hordes of insects attracted by the lights.

It is difficult to generalize about the housing requirements of tree frogs because they are such a diverse group. They require the usual aquarium-type enclosure, screen cover, optional lighting fixture if desired, and substrate. Enclosures for tree frogs should have some extra height as well as surface area. Most tree frogs move about by walking, leaping, and, in some instances, by what appears to be flying.

Arboreal species, and that includes most of them, should have sturdy branches on which to climb and perch, in addition to potted or planted live plants. Pet supply stores now carry an assortment of driftwood and artificial branches that blend nicely in such setups, or you can make your own. Some species prefer vines to hang on, so you can try these out and see how your tree frog likes them. A water bowl sunk into the substrate completes the picture; the water needs to be emptied and the bowl cleaned and refilled at least once a day.

In general, tree frogs eat the same kinds of insects that all other frogs eat, but they are more apt to find their food perched along a branch or shrub rather than on the ground.

There are forty different genera of tree frogs, and not all of these are popular as pets or even available in the pet trade. The following groups are among the most interesting or most likely to be available.

Cricket Frogs

Acris is a genus consisting of the cricket frogs. There are two species and about five subspecies of cricket frogs in the United States.

Northern Cricket Frog and Southern Cricket Frog

Cricket frogs are named for their ability to jump around rapidly like crickets. The northern cricket frog (*Acris crepitans*) and southern cricket frog (*Acris gryllus*) are small species, but their animated behavior dictates the need for a spacious enclosure. They eat a variety of small insects, such as half-grown crickets, flies, mealworms, and other bugs. This is a good, inexpensive species for the novice frog keeper if they are available. If you can maintain these frogs successfully, you can graduate to more exotic small frogs.

Cricket frogs prefer temperatures in the mid-60s to the mid-70s Fahrenheit. They need a well-planted terrarium with plenty of brush to hide in and a small pool of water, which should be changed daily. They are active primarily at night, and this is when you may hear them calling.

Leaf Frogs

The genus *Agalychnis*, the leaf frogs, has about ten species that range from southern Mexico through Central America to Ecuador along the Pacific coast of South America.

Red-Eyed Tree Frog

The ever-popular and hauntingly beautiful red-eyed tree frog (*Agalychnis callidyas*) has become the poster-frog of the save-the-rain-forest movement. Its photo can be found on calendars, posters, and in innumerable magazine articles and coffee-table books about tropical rain forests.

The red-eyed tree frog is found mainly on the Atlantic slopes and lowlands from central Mexico through northern Honduras and on the Caribbean slopes southward to Panama. This species lives in trees as high as 50 feet, but descends at nightfall during the rainy season to breed in ponds. They are often available in pet shops and from specialty breeders and importers.

This frog grows to a maximum s-v length of about 3 inches and is lime green above with sides that are bluish-green with cream bars and a cream-colored belly. Recently, a bright blue example of this frog was discovered, with orange feet and, of course, vivid bright red eyes.

One or a pair of these frogs need a spacious terrarium well-planted with broad-leafed plants, a substrate of sandy soil, and a water dish. These frogs like high humidity, which can be achieved by placing a piece of glass over one-third of the

Red-eyed tree frogs have become the poster-frogs for rain forest preservation.

screen cover. The remaining two-thirds should remain open to avoid poor ventilation and air stagnation. Misting several times a day will help maintain humidity and simulate their natural environment. This aspect of their care is essential, as they absorb all of their body water through their skin and will rapidly dehydrate, become inactive, and die.

Because these frogs normally live at great heights, they are more at home in a terrarium that is both spacious in area as well as higher than usual, such as a fifty-five- or sixty-gallon high tank. They require temperatures in the mid-70s Fahrenheit.

Experienced keepers say these frogs can become stressed rather easily, so they should not be handled unless absolutely necessary. It can take weeks for these frogs to get settled into a new home, and they should be not be stimulated excessively or disturbed during this period. In addition, it is advisable to feed only small numbers of insects at a time, making sure all the frogs get some. If you overfeed, the frogs will become overexcited and stressed.

This species is strictly nocturnal and spends the daylight hours "pasted" to the underside of a broad leaf frond or stuck in the corner of the terrarium. Set up a red nightlight bulb so you can observe their activity after dark.

Marsupial Frogs

The genus *Gastrotheca* encompasses about fifty species known collectively as marsupial frogs. The name literally means "stomach pouch." However, the scientist who named this group overlooked the fact that the pouch in which they rear their eggs and, in some species, their tadpoles, is located on their lower back, not the stomach—although this pouch may curve around to encompass part of the lateral abdomen. Many early scientists worked with preserved museum specimens only, which are not always in the best condition and certainly far from lifelike. In the case of this group of frogs, it was the presence of eggs and tadpoles in a pouch that involved the sides of the abdomen that undoubtedly led to this name. When the pouch is closed, it is exceedingly difficult to see the crescent-shaped, slitlike opening, especially in preserved specimens.

Marsupial frogs are found in Venezuela to northern Argentina, eastern Brazil, and throughout Panama. They are also found on the Pacific side of the Andes throughout Colombia and Ecuador.

Rio Bamba Marsupial Frog

The Rio Bamba marsupial frog (*Gastrotheca riobambae*) is common in gardens throughout large cities in Ecuador, as well as in the surrounding rain forest. Their color patterns are highly variable, but include mainly greens, tans, and bronzes in bars or blotches against a lighter tan or beige ground color. Some totally green frogs are also seen.

This is a chubby little frog, reaching s-v lengths of about 2½ to 3 inches, and is more terrestrial than most other tree frogs, living among low-lying vegetation near ponds and other bodies of water. It's right at home in large South American cities, existing in public parks as well as private courtyards and gardens, as long as there is a source of water available.

As a high-altitude species, the Rio Bamba marsupial frog prefers temperatures in the 60s to low 70s Fahrenheit, and does best in a true aqua-terrarium because it likes to swim. If you're using a decorative substrate, use leaf litter and moss for the land side and provide either a dish (1 to 2 inches deep) of water or a well-filtered partitioned side of water to a depth of 4 inches. Also provide rock formations, bark, and other natural structures for hiding places. The tank should be well ventilated but need not be heavily humidified.

These frogs are active night and day, and will eat a wide variety of suitably sized insects, including crickets, mealworms, small moths, and flies.

Two species of marsupial frogs; they carry their eggs in a pouch.

The most fascinating aspect of Rio Bamba marsupial frogs is their life history. After the eggs are laid and fertilized by the male, he assists the female, who uses her hind legs to roll them into the pouch on her lower back. There they remain until they become tadpoles or, in some species, fully formed froglets. The female delivers the live young herself, hanging in the water and bending her rear legs backward, inserting first one foot in the pouch and then the other, stretching it open, and allowing either a tadpole to enter the water or a fully formed froglet to emerge. The mother frog does this a hundred or more times until every last offspring in her pouch is freed.

Marsupial frog tadpoles are omnivores and will eat boiled lettuce, algae, aquatic plants, and vegetarian fish flake food crumbled to a suitable size. You can also try small aquatic organisms to feed them, although algae and other vegetable matter are more convenient.

True Tree Frogs

The genus *Hyla* is the largest and most diverse of the tree frog family, with some 300 or so living species, many of which are excellent candidates for both the novice and advanced frog and toad hobbyist. Because there are so many species spread over so much of the world, it is difficult to generalize about them. They are found throughout North, Central, and South America, the Caribbean, Eurasia, Europe, and coastal Africa north of the Sahara.

Known as the true tree frogs, these species have pads on their toes that enable them to adhere to the sides of trees, walls, aquariums, and branches. These sticky toe pads are their most distinctive feature. In addition, they have long, slender rear legs that enable them to propel themselves great distances—from branch to branch in fact, in search of a meal or a mate, or to escape danger. A number of true tree frogs make excellent pets.

The green tree frog has a beautiful voice.

Green Tree Frog

The green tree frog (*Hyla cinera*) is a U.S. species that is found from the tip of southern New Jersey, south along the Atlantic coastal plain through the Florida Keys, west through the Gulf States to southeastern Texas, and north to southern Illinois. There is also an isolated colony in south-central Missouri and this species has been introduced into northwestern Puerto Rico. Because of the bell-like quality of its voice, it is also known as the bell or cowbell frog.

This frog reaches a maximum s-v length of about 2¼ inches. It is usually bright green above with cream-colored longitudinal "racing stripes" along its sides, although these stripes are very short or nonexistent in some populations.

This frog and its close relatives, the gray tree frog (*Hyla versicolor*), bird voice tree frog (*Hyla avivoca*), and barking tree frog (*Hyla gratiosa*), need a large, tall enclosure that is well planted with plenty of sturdy branches for them to perch upon. A pool of water should be provided. They eat gut-loaded crickets, mealworms, wax worms, earthworms, and winged bugs such as small moths and flies.

Barking Tree Frog

The barking tree frog (*Hyla gratiosa*) is the largest native American tree frog, reaching s-v lengths of 2¾ inches. These frogs are readily

The barking tree frog is easily found in pet shops and makes a great "starter" frog.

available in local pet shops or can be collected personally. They are rarely captive-bred because they are so common and relatively inexpensive. They make excellent "starter" tree frogs, and, if well cared for, they can live for many years.

They'll need a tall aquarium with plenty of places to climb and a tight lid to keep them safe. They eat gut-loaded crickets, mealworms, moths, wax worms, and earthworms.

Australasian Tree Frogs

The genus *Litoria,* the Australasian tree frogs, contains more than 100 species found in Australia and Australasia, including Papua New Guinea, Indonesia, the Solomon Islands, and Timor. They have also been artificially introduced into New Zealand and New Caledonia.

Unquestionably the most readily available and most popular of this group of tree frogs is the White's tree frog (*Litoria caerulea*), with second place going to the white-lipped tree frog (*Litoria infrafrenata*). These frogs are sometimes available as wild-caught imports, but their popularity is so great that many frog professionals have been breeding them for years in the United States and Europe. Opting for captive-bred specimens (although somewhat more costly) means getting a better, healthier, and more robust frog that has not had to endure the stress of international air travel or come loaded with exotic parasites from the wild that would be difficult or impossible to control under captive conditions. More important, buying captive-born frogs helps to preserve these species in the wild.

White's Tree Frog

Given a proper diet and ideal surroundings, these frogs have been known to live for more than twenty years in captivity. White's tree frogs need a terrestrial aquarium that is well humidified, with the requisite pool or dish of water and a number of sturdy, somewhat larger or broader than usual perches—or better yet, shelves on which to sit. Substrate can consist of bark chips or sterile leaf litter, or just plain clean, white paper toweling, which should be changed daily. The water also needs to be changed daily. The glass walls of the aquarium should be washed, scraped, and cleaned two to three times a week.

The terrarium should be well ventilated with a screen cover top. Their preferred temperature range is 65 degrees to 75 degrees Fahrenheit.

Their color ranges from jade green to bluish-green, and all-blue animals are also available. Females reach 5 inches in s-v length, and males reach half that size. These are heavy-bodied frogs, one of a few frog species that become obese with overfeeding and lack of exercise in captivity. Older animals develop a fatty flap of tissue above the eyes, which can become so pronounced that it can partially or totally obstruct normal vision.

White's tree frogs have been known to live more than twenty years in captivity.

White's tree frogs are, however, well suited to captivity, and they are one of the few exotic species that are recommended to advanced keepers and newcomers alike. They are quite placid and tempting to hold, and will sit still on your shoulder or hand for varying periods of time. Of course, their behavior is unpredictable and they might hop off at a moment's notice. If they are not in a hurry, this species walks hand-over-hand in a rather slow and deliberate fashion—a very endearing trait.

White's tree frogs exude a bitter, toxic, whitish secretion to deter predators, so it is important to wash your hands thoroughly and immediately after handling them.

They eat a wide variety of insects, other frogs (including smaller members of their own species), small snakes, earthworms, and newborn mice. Dust food with a multivitamin-mineral powder or gut-load it beforehand.

Because of their toxic secretions and penchant for swallowing anything small that moves, it is best to keep only one or a pair of these frogs in a single enclosure. If you keep a pair, make sure the smaller male is at least half the size of the female so she will not be tempted to gobble him up.

The care, housing, and feeding requirements of white-lipped tree frogs, a close relative, are identical to that of White's tree frogs.

Cuban Tree Frogs

The genus Osteopilus has three similar species: the Cuban tree frog (*Osteopilus septentrionalis*), the Dominican tree frog (*Osteopilus dominicensis*), and the Savanna-La-Mar tree frog *(Osteopilus brunneus)*.

The Cuban tree frog is one of the most widely and commonly available frogs in the pet trade in the United States, and if you happen to live in or visit the southern half of the Florida peninsula you can collect these frogs just about anywhere, with the blessing of the local fish and game authorities. Because of Florida's proximity to Cuba, this frog routinely hitches rides on military aircraft and sea vessels, as well as private vessels plying the waters between Cuba and Key West, Florida. As a result, it has become a well-established species in most of the southern half of the state. It is now the largest tree frog in the United States, and environmental scientists fear it is crowding out or preying on smaller native species once occupying the niche it now inhabits.

These frogs are native to Cuba, the Bahamas, and the Cayman Islands, but have been introduced into Puerto Rico, St. Croix, and Hawaii as well as Florida. It is believed that the founder frogs of this species in Hawaii were escaped or deliberately released pets. As they are voracious predators and will eat insects, other frogs and lizards, and even hatchling birds in their nests, authorities are worried that this frog could upset the islands' ecological balance.

Cuban tree frogs are grayish-white. Females grow to an s-v length of 5 inches, and males grow to 3 inches. Captive animals have been known to live more than fifteen years.

They have huge toe pads, are extremely agile, and are voracious predators of any moving thing that

One way to make sure your frog lives a long, healthy life is to keep its enclosure securely covered so it cannot escape.

they are able to swallow. They can be found on the walls and doorways of houses at night, gobbling up insects attracted to household lights. During the day they rest.

Their preferred activity temperature is in the mid-70s to low-80s Fahrenheit. They can withstand short periods of colder temperatures, into the 50s or 60s Fahrenheit, but unless they are able to escape such cooler temperatures they do not endure for very long.

Part of their success in colonizing Florida and other habitats where they have been introduced is due to their noxious skin secretions, which keep them out of the mouths of predators. Because of their toxic secretions, you should be sure to wash thoroughly after handling them and not to touch your eyes or mouth before doing so.

Hawaii's Tree Frog Problem

Although no tree frog is native to Hawaii, colonies of alien Cuban tree frogs live in inland areas of the Kaneohe Koolau watershed on Oahu. Pacific tree frogs from the northwestern United States mainland also come in routinely on Christmas trees, and there are apt to be thriving colonies of them in Hawaii.

So far, Pacific tree frogs are allowed to be sold in Hawaiian pet stores, but Cuban tree frogs and barking dwarf tree frogs are illegal. Anyone convicted of importing illegal species into Hawaii faces a maximum penalty of $25,000 in fines and up to a year in jail!

For captive Cuban tree frogs, you will find no shortage of food items. They will eat the usual insect fare and the larger females will eat newborn mice.

These frogs are tough and hearty and require a well-planted terrarium with a screen cover, a water dish, and some sturdy perches or strong broad-leafed plants on which to hang. They should be misted several times a day or placed on an automatic misting system. They are excellent and inexpensive starter species for the new hobbyist, provided you don't live in Hawaii.

Chorus Frogs

This genus, *Pseudacris,* counts some thirteen species in North America.

Spring Peeper

The spring peeper (*Pseudacris crucifer*) and some dozen or so related species and subspecies are among the best-known frogs to millions of people in the United States, even though they have never seen them. They have, however, heard them. Every spring these small frogs begin to call by the hundreds of thousands, and although invisible to the untrained eye, their voice is well-known as the first sign of spring. Their calls are often mistaken for those of crickets. These are small frogs that eat tiny insects. A ten-gallon tank planted as a terrarium with branches to climb on can accommodate up to five of these small frogs.

Tropical Frogs

The tropical frogs include the number one on the hit parade of pet frogs: the horned frogs (*Ceratophrys*). Also known as Pac-Man frogs because of their large mouth and highly predatory nature, these frogs are being captive-bred and sold by the hundreds of thousands every year to frog lovers. They are relatively placid, "sit and wait" predators that stand stock-still most of the time. They are large and colorful.

Horned frogs are also capable of biting if you are not careful; they have large, sharp, front "snagging" teeth. If they snag you instead of the mouse or other food items you place in front of them, you are apt to get a nasty cut that should be thoroughly washed and immediately disinfected. However, if you are careful not to let these frogs confuse your fingers with their food (using long-handled tongs to feed them small mice is a good idea), you won't get injured.

There are a number of species that can be found in the captive-bred pet trade, including albino varieties. The most common are the Chaco or Cranwell's horned frog (*Ceratophrys cranwelli*), the Surinam horned frog (*Ceratophrys cornuta*), and the ornate horned frog (*Ceratophrys ornata*). The care and keeping of these and other members of the genus are basically the same.

Horned frogs should be housed singly because of their predatory nature. Because they are relatively inactive, a single animal can be comfortably housed in a five- or ten-gallon covered aquarium. Substrate can consist of either sphagnum moss, bark chips, sterile potting soil, or even plain paper toweling.

The brown Chaco horned frog on the left is normal and the yellow one is an albino.

These frogs prefer a warm and humid environment. A water dish should be present and part of the screen top can be covered with glass to help maintain humidity levels. Their preferred temperatures are between 75 and 85 degrees Fahrenheit; it may be necessary to use an undertank heating pad in colder weather. The water bowl and tank should be cleaned of any fecal material daily.

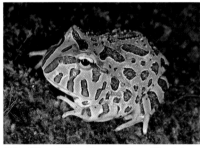

Like all horned frogs, the ornate horned frog is best housed alone.

Use long-handled tongs to feed small mice to your Surinam horned frog.

Discard and replace the substrate every three or four days; paper toweling substrate can easily be changed daily if necessary.

Smaller animals can be fed a variety of live bugs, including mealworms, earthworms, crickets, and the like. Larger frogs can be fed newborn mice or rats, graduating to somewhat larger or fuzzy mice or even young "hopper" mice as they grow. To maintain the frog's color, supplement or gut-load the food you give them with a vitamin-mineral powder. This is particularly important for growing young frogs, that should be fed daily. Adult frogs can be fed every two or three days, although adults of some species will not eat a good-sized meal more than once a week.

To avoid getting snagged on those teeth and to prevent the frog from ingesting any of its substrate (which can cause intestinal obstruction), it is a good idea to offer the frog live food dangling from the end of a long-handled pair of tongs or forceps. You can also help to prevent your frog from getting any intestinal problems by keeping it on a plain white paper toweling substrate.

Narrow-Mouthed Toads

The family of narrow-mouthed toads consists of about 300 species found throughout the southeastern United States, west to Texas and lower California, Mexico, and slightly more than half of South America, throughout sub-Saharan

Africa, Madagascar, eastern coastal India, Southeast Asia, China, and Australasia, including Indonesia and Papua New Guinea.

Tomato Frogs

One of the most popular genera in the pet trade are the tomato frogs, of which there are only three species, all from Madagascar: the Sambava tomato frog (*Dyscophus guineti*), the common tomato frog (*Dyscophus antogilii*), and the Antsouhy tomato frog (*Dyscophus insularis*). These plump, reddish frogs rarely exceed 3 or 4 inches in s-v length.

The brightest and largest of the trio is the common tomato frog, and is the species most commonly available as captive-bred in the United States. In fact, exports from Madagascar have effectively ceased due to concerns over dwindling populations, and although the problems faced by these frogs are not all due to the export pet trade (deforestation and other environmental ills are also a concern), a percentage of the losses are. Although wild-caught tomato frogs usually were sold loaded with parasites, which often killed them after a short while in a hobbyist's tank, captive-bred animals are virtually parasite-free and are far healthier.

These are hearty frogs that accept a wide variety of insects. The largest forms (over 3½ inches in s-v length) also eat newborn mice. They can withstand a wide

Tomato frogs are hearty animals and captive-bred frogs are easily available.

range of temperatures, from a low of 50 degrees to as hot as 90 degrees Fahrenheit, although an optimal range would be in the mid-70s. These frogs need a suitably sized aqua-terrarium (about one frog per five gallons of tank size), consisting of equal parts of land and shallow water (to a depth of about 3 inches). They require a screen cover and moderate humidity.

Spadefoot Toads

These are the legendary frogs that live on and under the dry plains and deserts, where they dig down a meter or more into the substrate, spinning themselves a cocoon-like coating of mucoid material to prevent dehydration, and then remaining dormant until the rains come. Scientists are not sure how they know it's raining while they are shrouded a meter below the surface, but it's believed they rip open and eat their cocoons and then dig themselves up when they hear the pitter-patter of the raindrops hitting the surface.

There are three genera most commonly obtained as pet frogs. The eastern spadefoot toad (*Scaphiopus holbrooki*) is found east of the Mississippi from central New England to the Florida Keys and inhabits well-drained sandy habitats. The western spadefoot toad (*Spea hammondi*) is found through arid habitats from south-central Canada through central Mexico. These are small, colorful frogs with a specialized protuberance on their rear feet, which they use to shovel their way underground. The third genus, *Pelobates*, consists of the European spadefoot toads (four species), found in Europe, Eurasia, and northwestern Africa.

These toads need a terrarium of loosely packed, sandy potting soil 3 to 4 inches in depth. The bottom layers need to be kept damp but the upper layers may be allowed to dry out. This is accomplished by inserting a 1-inch-diameter piece of plastic tubing into the soil just above the bottom layer and then used as a funnel through which you can pour enough water to dampen the bottom layer.

Spadefoot toads are a small species (2 to 3 inches s-v length) and require a diet of small insects such as half-grown crickets, mealworms, small earthworms, ants, termites, and the like. Spadefoots may be difficult to feed in some situations; this problem, along with their special habitat needs, does not make them a good beginner's frog.

The eastern spadefoot toad uses its rear feet to shovel its way underground.

Surinam Toads and African Clawed Frogs

This family includes the fully aquatic African clawed frogs and some strictly South American aquatic frogs known as Surinam toads, of which there are seven species. There are five genera and about thirty species of the clawed frogs in all. They are popular aquarium animals, although some species grow large enough to attack and eat tropical fish with which they may be housed.

Dwarf Clawed Frogs

There are five species of dwarf clawed frogs (*Hymenochirus sp.*), all from Africa. Several make suitable tankmates for community tropical fish such as guppies, swordtails, mollies, platys, and other fish that won't attack them.

These small, aquatic species do best in a well-covered, well-filtered, and well-aerated aquarium. Plants, rocks, and other hiding places should be provided. These frogs will eat small crickets kicking at the surface, tubifex worms, white worms, and other live aquarium foods.

The most prevalent in the U.S. pet trade is *Hymenochirus boettgeri*, that has the same common name as the other species: dwarf African clawed frog.

Surinam Toads

The Surinam toads (*Pipa sp.*) are large, fully aquatic frogs from South America. The most frequently available species is *Pipa pipa*. These frogs are best housed alone in an aquarium. It is possible to keep them with large goldfish or koi, but remember they are guaranteed to swallow any fish that they can fit in their mouth. They can be fed feeder tropical fish (but not feeder goldfish, which don't seem to agree with them), tubifex worms, crickets, mosquitoes, other aquatic insect larvae, and bait worms.

The aquarium should be well-filtered, aerated, and covered. A heater is necessary during colder weather; temperatures should be maintained between 75 degrees and 80 degrees Fahrenheit.

African Clawed Frogs

The African clawed frogs (*Xenopus sp.*) can reach 4 to 5 inches in s-v length. These frogs are commercially bred in captivity for laboratory research, with some animals diverted to the pet trade. They are fully aquatic and are best kept alone in a well-covered, vigorously filtered, and well-aerated aquarium. A heater may be used in winter to maintain water temperature between 75 and 85 degrees Fahrenheit.

Surinam toads are fully aquatic and are best housed alone in an aquarium.

African clawed frogs foul their water quickly, so be ready for lots of water changes. The light one here is an albino.

These frogs foul their water rather quickly, so be prepared to do partial water and filter material changes frequently and complete water changes every seven to ten days. They will eat feeder guppies and other tropical fish, tubifex worms, earthworms, and insects that are tossed in the water in their view. Be sure to remove drowned, uneaten insects with a net.

The most common species of large African clawed frog found in pet shops and dealer lists is *Xenopus laevis*. It is also raised for laboratory use.

True Frogs

This group has the rather silly name of true frogs, which suggests that all other frogs are "false." In any event, these are typical semi-aquatic frogs that structurally resemble one another. This is a very widespread and very large group of frogs with more than 700 species in more than fifty genera. They are found throughout North, Central, and the northern third of South America, throughout Europe east to China, through sub-Saharan Africa and the Middle East, on the Indian subcontinent east through southern Asia, Indonesia, Papua New Guinea, and Australasia. They are absent, except as artificially introduced, in the West Indian and Pacific Oceanic islands.

Most members of the family are semi-aquatic, but a few species are primarily terrestrial—entering the water periodically to breed, escape enemies, thermoregulate, or find food.

The Rana True Frogs

Some common "true" frogs are fairly common in the pet trade.

American Bullfrog

The American bullfrog (*Rana cate-sebeiana*) is the largest of the North American native frog species. It gets its common name from its call, which sounds like the bellow of a bull. Originally found east of the Rocky Mountains, this giant species has spread west to the Pacific coast, where it is preying on and competing with local species. It has been introduced worldwide and can be found in such diverse locations as Italy and other parts of Europe, Cuba, many West Indian islands, and Hawaii. It was originally imported into

The American bullfrog is the largest native North American frog.

these areas to be farmed as a source of frogs' legs for food, but has escaped and established itself in the countryside surrounding these breeding operations. Bullfrogs have created havoc for local species wherever they've escaped into the wild.

The American bullfrog is a semiaquatic species and spends as much or more time in the water as on land. It often remains submerged just below the surface with eyes and nostrils protruding. It needs a large, semiaquatic or aqua-terrarium setup with significant water depth and land to haul out onto. This frog is a strong jumper, and its enclosure must have a secured screen cover—an unsecured cover could probably be pushed off by this species. The water side needs to be well-filtered and allow for easy water changes, which must be done frequently.

Male adult bullfrogs can reach s-v lengths of 6 to 7 inches; females are smaller at maximum lengths of 5 inches. This frog is a voracious predator that eats other frogs, including smaller members of its own species; reptiles, including snakes and even baby alligators; small mammals; birds; and insects. Bullfrogs have even been observed shooting straight out of the water to catch airborne insects such as butterflies, moths, and large mosquitoes. They have also been seen catching and devouring small bats this way. Bullfrogs prefer ingesting and swallowing their prey under water and often submerge before eating prey caught on land or in the air. Preferred temperature ranges from the mid-60s to the 70s Fahrenheit, although higher and lower temperatures can be tolerated.

Although relatively common and inexpensive, bullfrogs require spacious enclosures or even outdoor ponds to survive long in a captive situation. For this reason, they are not recommended for beginners; there are more interesting, more manageable, and smaller ranid species to choose from.

The common leopard frog is widely bred for use in research and as a pet.

Common Leopard Frog

The common leopard frog (*Rana pipiens*) is a pretty, spotted frog with patterns and color combinations that depend on the animal's geographic location. It is found throughout North America, but populations of some subspecies are declining. Because this frog is commercially captive-bred for educational and research use, it is relatively inexpensive.

This is an active species and is much smaller than the bullfrog—measuring about 3 inches s-v length. They require a semiaquatic aquarium with a strong cover, as these frogs are excellent jumpers. Temperature should be in the mid-70s Fahrenheit. They eat a wide variety of suitable size insects and make an excellent starter frog.

Wood Frog

The wood frog (*Rana sylvatica*) is a small species of common terrestrial frog that requires a terrarium with a water dish. It eats small insects, is easy to care for, and makes an excellent starter frog for a woodland terrarium with a leaf-litter substrate. It tolerates a wide range of temperatures, from as low as 50 degrees to as high as 80 degrees Fahrenheit. A cover is, of course, required.

The wood frog's natural range in the northern reaches of Canada puts it just inside the Arctic Circle. It is being studied so we can better understand its ability to actually freeze and then thaw out unscathed.

The wood frog is very hardy and can survive far into northern Canada.

African Pyxie Bullfrogs

The name "pyxie" derives from the Greek word *pyxsis,* which means "small box." The original describer of this genus, *Pyxicephalus,* thought this frog's head was reminiscent of a small box. (The Latin word *cephalus* means "head.")

Pyxie Bullfrog

The pyxie or African pyxie bullfrog (*Pyxicephalus adspersus*) is anything but pixyish. When fully grown, males of this species can reach 10 inches in s-v length, females about 5 to 6 inches. These popular giants are commonly bred in captivity and can be found from mail-order dealers, breeders, and occasionally, in pet shops. They are simply called pyxie frogs by most hobbyists.

They are a quiet, rather sedentary species that, because of their bulk, can hop rather than jump. They spend a majority of their time dug into drier substrates in the wild. Unlike the American bullfrog, pyxie bullfrogs are primarily a terrestrial species and require a terrarium with a suitably sized dish of water for the occasional soak. A pyxie bullfrog will generally foul its water bowl with every single visit, so the water should be changed whenever this occurs.

In captivity, they should be housed alone in a large enclosure. A single full-grown male can be comfortably housed in a twenty-gallon aquarium tank. You can use a paper toweling substrate if desired, but your frog will be more at home with a soil, bark, or litter substrate into which it can burrow. The enclosure should be maintained in the 75- to 85-degree Fahrenheit range.

The pyxie bullfrog is no pixie. This is a big frog!

Although it is unlikely that this hefty creature could jump clear out of a tank that is 10 or more inches high, a screen cover is still a good idea. It also prevents your frog from getting any unwanted attention from a family cat or dog.

These frogs will eat anything they can swallow, including a wide variety of larger insects such as full-grown crickets, super worms, and even mice. Large captive animals have even been fed small rats and baby chicks. They are cannibalistic and should not be housed with any other frogs, especially smaller ones. Even baby pyxie bullfrogs will try to eat their brothers and sisters, so all must be kept in solitary quarters.

They also have three sharp teeth on their lower jaw and will not hesitate to bite the hand that feeds them if you come too close. Feeding is best accomplished with a pair of long-handled tongs, using techniques similar to those recommended for horned frogs. While frequent handling of any frog is discouraged, pyxie bullfrogs can be picked up around the midriff or you can use an extremely large net or even a birdseed or similar scoop to move or block a frog when you need to do maintenance on its enclosure.

These are impressive, hearty, and easy-to-care for frogs, and are recommended for the moderately advanced amateur.

Mantella Frogs

Mantella frogs are colorful, popular, interesting small frogs that reach a maximum s-v length of 1½ inches. These colorful frogs are the equivalent of Madagascar's dart-poison frog, and the island nation of Madagascar is the only place on Earth where these species live. Like dart-poison frogs, they produce a toxic skin secretion which, while not as deadly, still dictates the use of safe handling precautions.

The mantella frogs are dwindling in numbers, and what few reach the United States are the subject of intense captive-breeding programs by professionals so that the hobby interest can be sustained without taking any more of these tiny frogs away from their natural habitat. There are some nine species recognized by science, but scientists are learning new things about this group of animals all the time.

Mantella frogs do not have a common name and are just called mantella frogs, even though Mantella is the genus part of its scientific name. Among the species most commonly seen in the hobbyist or pet trade are: the golden mantella (*Mantella aurantica*), an all golden or red frog; the painted mantella (*Mantella madagascarensis*), brightly colored with splotches of lime green, gold, red, and even turquoise on a black background; the Fology mantella (*Mantella laevigata*), which is even more brightly "painted" than the painted mantella; and the green mantella (*Mantella virdis*), which is mostly lime green with a black face mask similar to a raccoon's mask.

Keep mantellas of the same species together in a single enclosure, but do not keep different *Mantella* species in one cage. As small but territorial frogs, they need approximately five gallons of tank space to one frog. A group of four, therefore, could be housed comfortably in a twenty-gallon aquarium tank laid out as a jungle terrarium. It should be well planted with a waterfall or plastic water dish at one end, with plenty of hiding places such as "caves." Caves can be constructed by using half a coconut

This is a brown mantella frog (Mantella betsileo).

shell, store-bought bark caves over wood, or even the bottoms cut from two-liter or one-liter plastic soda bottles. Water bowls should allow these tiny frogs easy access and exit, and should be changed at least daily to prevent their toxic skin secretions from building up in the water.

Maintain temperatures between 65 degrees and 75 degrees Fahrenheit. Below 65 degrees they become dormant and at temperatures above 80 degrees they become stressed.

They are great climbers and jumpers, so a secure, tightly fitted screen cover is a necessity. Humidity can be maintained by misting or using an automatic rainmaking device several times a day. Part of the screen cover can be closed with a sheet of plate glass to hold humidity in. A full-spectrum fluorescent fixture is also advisable. (It will also help your live plants grow.) Do not, however, rely on a full aquarium hood as a cover, because these small frogs have a way of climbing out into the light fixture or through tiny spaces and escaping. It is preferable, therefore, to place a hood or reflector strip fixture atop a tightly fitted screen cover.

Mantella frogs need to be fed daily or at least every other day. These frogs will die without frequent feedings, so if this schedule will not fit into your lifestyle or if you must travel and do not have an alternate caretaker at home, mantella frogs are not a good choice for you. As with the dart-poison frogs, you need to ensure a steady, continual source of small live feeder insects, including fruit flies, pinhead crickets, ants, termites, and the like. Bugs should be lightly dusted with a suitable vitamin-mineral supplement at least once or twice a week.

Properly fed, cared for, and housed, these frogs make hearty pets and are recommended for the advanced amateur with the facilities and commitment to take care of them.

Chapter 8

Frogs and Toads in the Wild

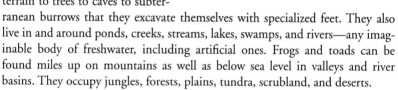

Frogs and toads inhabit virtually every habitat the Earth has to offer—from surface terrain to trees to caves to subterranean burrows that they excavate themselves with specialized feet. They also live in and around ponds, creeks, streams, lakes, swamps, and rivers—any imaginable body of freshwater, including artificial ones. Frogs and toads can be found miles up on mountains as well as below sea level in valleys and river basins. They occupy jungles, forests, plains, tundra, scrubland, and deserts.

The only place you won't find them is in the ocean; no frog or toad can tolerate full-strength seawater due to their permeable skin. Contact with saltwater would quickly poison them because, unlike reptiles and many marine species, they have no means of excreting excess salt. Still, a few species are found in brackish or estuarine habitats. These include the marine or giant tropical toad (*Bufo marinus*), which is also called the cane toad in Australia, and the European natterjack toad (*Bufo calamita*). There is, however, no need to duplicate such habitats for these species in captivity. Their presence in brackish or low-salinity environments is an aberration that they can tolerate but that they do not require.

Size and Growth

The largest frog in the world is the West African (Goliath) bullfrog (*Conraua goliath*), which, when measured from the tip of its snout to its cloacal vent, can reach a foot or more in length. Other large frogs include marine/cane toad, the Colorado River toad (*Bufo alvarius*), the South American Blomberg's toad (*Bufo blombergi*), and the American bullfrog. Male African bullfrogs can reach s-v lengths of 10 inches. They are often nicknamed "pyxie" frogs because of their scientific name (*Pyxicephalus adspersus*), but this has nothing to do with their eventual size. The other giants of the frog world also grow up to 8 to 10 inches in s-v length.

Among the smallest frogs are the dart-poison frogs, like this Amazonian.

However, most frogs and toads reach nowhere near these sizes, and range from miniature species of less than a quarter of an inch s-v length to midrange sizes of 4 to 6 inches.

From Tadpole to Adult

An interesting paradox about frog and toad tadpoles is that as they develop into fully formed frogs, they actually grow shorter rather than longer. This is because tadpoles have tails that disappear as they grow into fully formed, four-legged adults. Thus a 2-inch tadpole, when it finishes transforming into a baby froglet, may be only half an inch in s-v length. The frog then starts to grow again, only this time it is its body that becomes longer and larger. The paradoxical frog is an actual species that got its name for just this reason—this species begins life as a particularly large tadpole that metamorphoses into a particularly tiny froglet.

The amount of time it takes a frog or toad egg to transform into a tadpole and a tadpole into a fully formed froglet or toadlet depends on the species as well as a variety of external factors, including water conditions, temperature, and availability of food. Some species born into temporary pools, even puddles or rain deposits in the cup of leaves, metamorphose quite rapidly. If they didn't, they would be doomed to die without developing into an air-breathing land, aquatic, or semiaquatic adult. Thus, it can take anywhere from a few weeks to two or three months for some species to metamorphose. And a few species become tadpoles in the summer or early fall, over-winter as larval tadpoles, and then metamorphose the following spring.

Reproduction in Frogs and Toads

There is no more fascinating aspect of frog and toad study than the way they mate, breed, lay their eggs, and develop their larvae or tadpoles. The study of frog and toad reproduction is characterized by one word: "exceptions." No single order or group of related animals, in which the majority conform to a fairly uniform means of reproduction, have as many different reproductive processes as the frogs and toads. They are utterly and without a doubt the most fascinating and most diverse group of animals when it comes to mating, reproduction, and life history.

The Standard Reproduction Process

It is hard for anyone familiar with all the exceptions to believe that there is a norm or standard; however, some reproductive "rules" do prevail. The vast majority of female frogs find mates by answering the mating calls of the males during the breeding season. When a mating occurs, usually in the water, the male grasps the female by placing his front legs around either her waist or her chest under her front legs. This grasp is known as amplexsus. He then proceeds to squeeze the unfertilized eggs out of the female, depositing sperm and fertilizing them all at once. The eggs develop in the water, either floating in strings or clumps or attaching themselves to pieces of vegetation or rock formations.

Frogs show a lot of diversity in their reproduction habits. These marsupial frogs carry their eggs in a pouch.

The single-celled egg starts dividing and it soon becomes a multicellular sphere, transforming itself into a tadpole or larva. Now begins the second stage of a frog or toad's development. The tadpoles are strictly aquatic organisms and, as a rule, develop in the water. Tadpoles eat vegetable matter, animal matter, or a combination of both, and many species of tadpole are cannibalistic as well.

Eventually, the tadpole starts to sprout legs—first the front legs and then the hind legs. At the same time, the long tail is reabsorbed and disappears and the gills are lost in favor of lungs—although all frogs and toads can also breathe through their skin. Many species still retain some vestiges of their tail as they emerge onto land, but this is quickly lost. This process is known as metamorphosis, a word that literally means "structural change." At this point, the newly minted froglets or toadlets, as the case may be, emerge from the water and are ready to lead an amphibious existence, on land and in the water.

Exceptions to the Rules

As noted earlier, there are many exceptions to the "standard" process. First, let's consider the fact that frogs deposit their eggs in the water. For the vast majority of frogs and toads, this can be either permanent or temporary, standing or even running water. But then there are frog moms that deposit their eggs in natural or specially constructed basins of water. There are tree frogs that deposit their eggs in the cups of leaves or aerial plants and others that use standing water accumulated in tree holes.

The strawberry dart-poison frog (*Dendrobates pumilio*) first lays five to ten eggs on a horizontal leaf; both the male and female visit them regularly and keep them moist by urinating on them. When they become tadpoles, the female carries each one to its own individual water bath fashioned out of the deep leaves (cupolas) of nearby aerial plants. She places a single egg in the cup of a bromeliad or epiphyte (air) plant, and returns to each tadpole and deposits several nonfertile eggs for the tadpole to feed on. This is but one of the most remarkable discoveries in the fascinating world of frog and toad behaviors, and no one could believe that these lowly animals confer this kind of parental care on their offspring when it was first observed in a greenhouse population of these frogs.

Another unusual reproductive activity has been demonstrated by the Australian gastric brooding frog (*Rheobatrachus silus*). This species was discovered just before it became extinct. This remarkable frog, and a close relative now also thought to be extinct, laid their eggs in the water, where they were fertilized and then swallowed by the female. The eggs and tadpoles completed their development in the stomach, and the baby froglets emerged from the mother's mouth some time later. The biochemical means this species used to turn her stomach into a womb will probably never be known.

Frog Metamorphosis

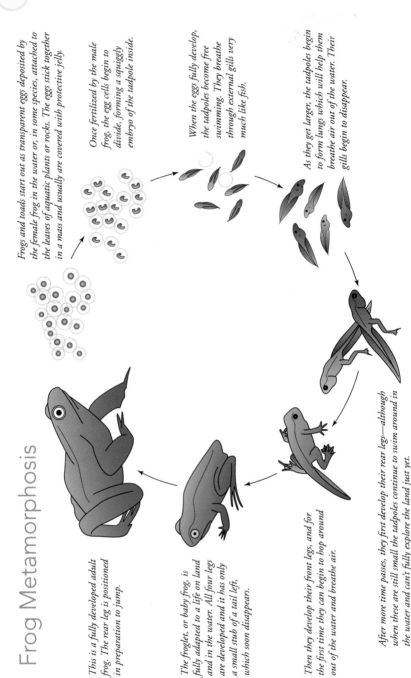

Frogs and toads start out as transparent eggs deposited by the female frog in the water or, in some species, attached to the leaves of aquatic plants or rocks. The eggs stick together in a mass and usually are covered with protective jelly.

Once fertilized by the male frog, the egg cells begin to divide, forming a squiggly embryo of the tadpole inside.

When the eggs fully develop, the tadpoles become free swimming. They breathe through external gills very much like fish.

As they get larger, the tadpoles begin to form lungs which will help them breathe air out of the water. Their gills begin to disappear.

After more time passes, they first develop their rear legs—although when these are still small the tadpoles continue to swim around in the water and can't fully explore the land just yet.

Then they develop their front legs, and for the first time they can begin to hop around out of the water and breathe air.

The froglet, or baby frog, is fully adapted to a life on land and in the water. All four legs are developed and it has only a small stub of a tail left, which soon disappears.

This is a fully developed adult frog. The rear leg is positioned in preparation to jump.

There are also species that deposit their eggs in foam nests they build on or near ponds and streams without actually entering the water. And then there is the Surinam toad, a strictly aquatic frog that incubates its eggs under a sheath of epithelial tissue on its back.

There are yet other species that deposit their eggs on damp ground (sometimes in excavated nests). The eggs are left at a specific time, so that they will develop into aquatic larvae in time for flooding, when they will be carried into the water in runoff. When the flooding does not occur as anticipated, some species carry the tadpoles to the water themselves by allowing them to wriggle up onto their legs and back.

The South American marsupial frogs, a large group of tree frogs (*Gastrotheca sp.*), have a dorso-lateral pouch on their backs. After fertilization, the female carries the eggs in the pouch, where they develop either into free-living tadpoles or fully formed frogs. When they are ready to be liberated, the female stretches open the pouch with her hind legs, allowing her babies to drop out.

The male Darwin's frog (*Rhinoderma darwini*) carries the eggs in his vocal pouch and the male of the European midwife toad (*Alytes obstetricians*) also gets into the act by carrying the eggs pasted onto his hind legs until they develop.

Frog Communication

Frogs are the only amphibians with a true voice, although salamanders have been heard to make clicking sounds. Frog calls are famous for their variety, resonance, and resemblance to other sounds. The call of the common American green frog, for example, sounds like someone strumming on a banjo! When frogs call in unison this is called a chorus, and such night sounds are a cardinal sign that life still exists in the darkness long after others have gone to sleep.

Frogs have a variety of different calls, and no two species of frog have the same call or call on the same sound frequency. Calls are used by both males and females, although the loudest calls are made by the males when seeking a mate—an advertising call. Males that are mated by other males will emit a special call known as a release call, telling the amorous suitor, in effect, to get lost. And if one frog gets in trouble or is attacked, it will emit a distress call, warning all frog brethren in the area that something bad is happening. There are even frogs that can call underwater.

Frog call CDs are available, and you can also hear a variety of them

The U.S. National Biological Survey uses the distinctive call of frogs to determine whether a particular species still lives in areas where it existed previously.

This marine toad is making itself heard.

on the Internet. Many scientists spend their careers studying these calls, their sound frequencies, and their significance.

The deafening call of some French frogs is alleged to have been the final straw, causing the outbreak of the French Revolution in 1789. According to this tale, the French nobility were being kept awake by the frogs on July 12, 1789. The next evening, they ordered their servants to stay up all night and whenever the servants heard the frogs start to call, they were to slap the water with sticks and paddles to shut them up. This degrading request was the ultimate insult to be heaved upon the peasants, and the next day, July 14th, they stormed the Bastille! Whether this story is true or not is a matter of conjecture, but the timing is right: In France, the first two weeks of July are prime frog-calling time.

Hibernation and Aestivation

When conditions at the surface become either too hot or too cold, frogs that live in areas of climatic extremes cannot migrate to more hospitable environments the way fish, birds, and some mammals do. Instead they resort to one of two things: They either hibernate to escape the extreme cold or they aestivate to escape excessive heat.

Hibernation Practices Vary

When the temperature starts to drop, frog activity levels begin to drop along with it. They pass their last meal and then eat no more, their heart and respirations slow, and they become more and more lethargic until they move no more. Although a scant few species can survive total freezing, thanks to their ability to manufacture a glycerol-based cellular antifreeze, most frogs and toads dig into the substrate—whether it's at the bottom of a pond or on the forest floor—to levels just below the eventual frost line and wait for favorable conditions to return at the surface.

The most cold-tolerant species of frogs live in North America. The wood frog (*Rana sylvatica*), the spring peeper (*Pseudacris crucifer*), the gray tree frog

(*Hyla versicolor*), and the boreal toad (*Bufo boreas*) emerge from hibernation months before other species, even while there may still be snow on the ground. The gray tree frog extends well into Manitoba, Canada; the wood frog as far north as the Yukon and Northwest Territories and the Alaskan tundra, just inside the Arctic Circle. Spring peepers and boreal toads extend far north into Canada as well.

These "freeze-tolerant" species are able to manufacture excessive amounts of *glycerol,* which serves as a cellular antifreeze of sorts and prevents cells from freezing completely under the coldest conditions. These species survive months of freezing with about 65 percent of their total body water as ice, and have been found encased in blocks of ice, only to be slowly thawed and fully recovered.

While freezing of cells is not a problem, the cells often rupture when thawing out, and this is what causes the death of an organism that is frozen alive.

Aestivating Species

Obviously, subtropical and tropical species from the American south to the equator do not hibernate, but these species practice another sort of inactivity to prevent their metabolic collapse during periods of excessive heat: They dig in to the cooler substrate or damp earth and *aestivate.*

Frogs and toads also aestivate during periods of excessive dryness to conserve precious body water until the rain reappears. Among the species that do this regularly are many desert and plains frogs, including the American spadefoot toads and the Australian water-holding frogs (*Cyclorana sp.*).

The boreal toad emerges from hibernation months before most other species.

The biology of hibernation—lowered metabolism, diminished circulation, and a curtailed need for oxygen and carbon dioxide elimination via breathing during extreme cold—is fairly well understood. The means by which frogs do this under conditions of extreme heat and aridity is not as well documented.

Releasing Frogs and Toads into the Wild

In a word, *don't*. Allowing captive frogs or toads to escape into the wild or deliberately releasing them is an irresponsible act that could have dire consequences for other wild frogs and toads and for the environment. Never consider releasing any nonnative species into a new habitat. Chances are, it is poorly adapted for the habitat and will die, and that is irresponsible. But if that species does prosper, it could compete with, crowd out, or quite possibly even eat other frogs, toads, and species it was not intended by nature to harm.

There are many examples of the havoc caused by such releases or escapes throughout the world. The American bullfrog, for example, uses up natural resources intended for other animals worldwide, including some in the United States.

Another giant species, the marine toad, has caused similar problems. The toad was deliberately released on many islands, including Hawaii and Australia. This is a tough species, reproduces at enormous rates, and has established itself at the expense of native species, which in many places it gobbles up with abandon. The overabundance of released African clawed frogs in California waters is yet another example.

The Cuban tree frog is threatening native frog populations in southern Florida.

South American dart-poison frogs, Cuban tree frogs, Japanese wrinkled frogs, and American bullfrogs all have been deliberately or accidentally introduced into Hawaii. The bullfrog has even earned itself a Hawaiian name: *poloka lana*. The Cuban tree frog, which found its way to south Florida, can now be found throughout the southern half of the state, and native tree frogs have either died out or have become extremely scarce as a result.

And if you ever contemplate re-releasing a native frog back into its own habitat, it is also wise to reconsider. In captivity, frogs and toads may pick up and become immune to bacteria and viruses that wild living frogs and toads have never encountered. It is conceivable that a pathogen introduced by a released captive could eradicate an entire population of wild frogs. In fact, infectious diseases may well be responsible for some notable frog disappearances.

There is no use tempting fate by such well-intentioned but misguided actions. If you can no longer keep a frog or toad, give it away—back to the pet shop, a local school,

These Malayan leaf frogs are easily camouflaged. Trade in international species is regulated through CITES.

a zoo, or a friend. If you try, you will find someone who is willing to adopt your unwanted frog.

However, the careful controlled release of captive-bred species back into their natural or native habitat is done occasionally to repopulate areas where such species once existed but have disappeared. Such release programs, however, are done under the strictest scientific and veterinary medical supervision. Professional biologists, veterinarians, conservationists, environmental scientists, and fish and game professionals are all consulted in such planned events. An individual who thinks he can engage in such a program on his own is simply courting disaster.

The release of not only frogs but also the water captive frogs are kept in could also be responsible for introducing harmful microorganisms into the environment. An example of this recently occurred in Japan, where native frogs, for the first time, were found to be infected with the chytrid fungus. This fungus is a frog killer that survives in water (see the box on page 118).

> **TIP**
>
> The U.S. and international list of endangered, threatened, or species of special concern changes rapidly. You can find the updated legal status of endangered frogs and toads at www.globalamphibians.org.

Deadly Fungus

In Central and South America, scientists have documented the apparent extinction of at least sixty-five species of frogs and toads in recent years. The culprit was determined to be the *chytrid fungus*, which attacks frog skin and teeth and produces a dangerous toxin that causes frogs to die.

It is spreading worldwide, from Central and South America to as far away as Australia and more recently, Japan. An emergency joint statement was issued in January 2007 by sixteen organizations, including the Japanese Society of Zoo and Wildlife Medicine, the Herpetological Society of Japan, and World Wide Fund for Nature Japan. The statement calls on frog keepers not to release the water that kept dead frogs into the outdoor environment—thus helping to check the spread of the fungus. It also calls on frog importers and sellers to ensure their frogs are not infected with the chytrid fungus. In fact, any water holding captive frogs should only be drained into sewerage or dry ground, and never into local streams, canals, lakes, or swamps.

The fungus is believed to have originated in African clawed frogs that entered worldwide trade as long ago as the 1930s for use in pregnancy testing for humans. When they were no longer

Frogs, Toads, and the Law

In some places in the United States, some species of frogs and toads are protected by the federal Endangered Species Act or by various state laws. Worldwide, by far the most wide-sweeping international regulation of rare, endangered, and threatened populations of frogs is the Convention on Trade in Endangered Species (CITES). This is a United Nations–sponsored organization, of which many of the most important consumer nations are signatories, including the United States. Thus, if a species of frog from India, for example, is on the Convention's endangered species list, it cannot be imported into the United States without CITES documents detailing everything about the animal.

needed for this purpose, the frogs continued to be used in reproductive research as well as to study the antibiotic nature of their skin secretions—which prevents them from getting sick from the fungus itself but doesn't stop them from carrying it to environments that are home to other species without these defenses. Ill-conceived release of captive African clawed frogs, including those kept as aquarium pets, has resulted in their establishment in the wild in the United States, Britain, and South America, and perhaps elsewhere, and has caused the fungus to spread.

The spread of the fungus has also been linked to climate change as a result of global warming. The higher temperatures resulting from global warming add more water vapor to the air, which in turn forms a cloudy cover that causes cooler days and warmer nights. Temperatures that favor the spread of frog-killing chytrid fungus (63 to 77 degrees Fahrenheit) occur more frequently as a result of these climate changes. These findings illustrate the fragile and delicate balance between life on Earth and the climate. Frog-related discoveries are causing scientists and politicians who had been skeptical about global warming and climate change to revise their positions.

CITES is a permit system of sorts, but it is really a means by which trade is tracked and, if necessary, checked.

In cases where a shipment is suspect or the species is severely endangered, the CITES authority is likely to refuse documentation. If it is shipped anyway, the United States considers it smuggled contraband and will confiscate the animals, arrest the consignees inside the United States, and prosecute them and the shippers (if possible) for criminal violations. Other nation signatories that catch smugglers inside their borders will also prosecute them for violation of the international treaty that they have agreed to honor.

A domestic U.S. law called the Lacy Act makes it a federal crime to cause the interstate transport of an endangered species without a special permit from the

U.S. Department of the Interior. This law also applies to the movement of any animal or plant that is moved from a state where its possession may be legal to one where it is not legal, and it is triggered at U.S. borders when foreign endangered or illegal species are concerned, as well.

Protecting Frogs and Toads

It is only recently that environmental scientists have discovered that our frog friends are in peril and their numbers are dwindling or disappearing completely. In just ten years, Australian gastric brooding frogs and the spectacular Costa Rican golden toad have become extinct for no readily apparent reason, although everything from the hole in the ozone layer (causing excessive UV radiation), global warming and other climate change, to acid rain has been implicated.

Among the U.S. species in serious trouble are the Houston toad (*Bufo houstonensis),* the Puerto Rican crested toad (*Peltophryne lemur*), the Colorado River toad, the Cascades frog (*Rana cascadae*), the tailed frog, the Anderson's or Pine-Barrens tree frog, (*Hyla andersoni*), and the Western spadefoot toad (*Spea hammondi*). Even one of America's most common species, the ubiquitous leopard frog, is imperiled in many locations. This shortage of leopard frogs has been blamed on local wholesale collection of the species for use in laboratories and for student dissection.

Many scientists consider amphibians as sentinel species—proverbial canaries in the coal mine and suggest their decline foretells greater danger for people. They blame humans for destroying frog habitats with toxic waste, garbage and sewage, heavy metal residues, radioactive wastes, pesticides, herbicides, and chemical fertilizers, as well as creating conditions ripe for potentially fatal infectious diseases.

Sadly, greater-than-normal numbers of deformed and multiple-limbed abnormal frogs are being discovered in the wild. No one is quite sure of the causes of these deformities or if they are even a part of the declining frog problem. But while the debate rages on, frogs continue to disappear.

Kermit the Frog, in the book *One Frog Can Make a Difference,* probably said it best: "If you wait until the frogs and toads have croaked their last to take some action, you've missed the point."

The decline of amphibians may foretell our own decline. Our pets may also be our protectors—if we can also protect them.

Learning More About Your Frog or Toad

Some Good Books

Bartlett, Richard, and Patricia Bartlett, *Terrarium and Cage Construction and Care*, Barron's Educational Series, 1999.

Conant, Roger, and Joseph T. Collins, *Reptiles and Amphibians: Eastern/Central North America*, 3rd ed. (Peterson Field Guide Series), Houghton Mifflin Company, 1993.

Duellman, William F, and Linda Trueb, *Biology of Amphibians*, Johns Hopkins University Press, 1994.

Grenard, Steve, *Amphibians: Their Care and Keeping*, Howell Book House, 1999.

Stebbins, Robert C., and Nathan W. Cohen, *A Natural History of Amphibians*, Princeton University Press, 1997.

Wright, Kevin M., and Brent R. Whitaker, *Amphibian Medicine and Captive Husbandry*, Krieger Publishing Company, 2001.

Magazines

Reptiles Magazine
P.O. Box 6040
Mission Viejo, CA 92690
(800) 876-9112
www.reptilesmagazine.com

Internet Resources

There are numerous web sites devoted to frogs and toads. Thanks to giant search engines, you can find these with relative ease. Key words for searching include anura, anurans, amphibians, frogs, salientia, toads, tadpoles, and herpetology. Also use species and family names of a species you are interested, such as "Bufo" for all bufonid toads or *Bufo marinus* for that particular species of toad.

You can also search Yahoogroups for discussion forums, where you can ask questions or provide answers on frogs and toads you have in common with others.

American Society of Ichthyologists and Herpetologists
www.asih.org
This group publishes a journal, is involved in conservation projects, and has other activties.

The BioDiversity Group
www.thebdg.org
The main subject of this site is the conservation and captive breeding of a small group of South American frogs belonging to the *Dendrobates, Phyllobates, Colostethus,* and related genera.

Exploratorium: Frog Links
www.exploratorium.edu/frogs/links.html
This site from the Exploratorium science museum in San Francisco offers links to a wide variety of information on frog species, forums, environmental issues, and other topics.

Herp Societies and Rescues
www.anapsid.org/societies/
Joining a group of people with like-minded interests and exchanging information as well as benefiting from the publications of such groups can be extremely important. The latest list of herpetology societies and clubs by state can be found here.

Society for the Study of Amphibians and Reptiles
www.ssarherps.org
Society members receive both *Journal of Herpetology* and *Herpetological Review.*

The Union of Concerned Scientists
www.ucsusa.org/ucs/about/
The Union of Concerned Scientists is a science-based nonprofit group working for a healthy environment. And check out the Web site for the latest global environmental threats.

The Whole Frog Project
froggy.lbl.gov/
This is a three-dimensional reconstruction of frog anatomy—a virtual frog dissection kit.

Reptile and Amphibian Veterinarians

Association of Reptilian and Amphibian Veterinarians
www.arav.org/Directory.htm
This online ARAV membership directory lists members by state in the United States and by country or geographical region elsewhere in the world.

The Herp Vet Connection
www.herpvetconnection.com
This site has a list of veterinarians recommended by reptile and amphibian owners worldwide, as well as links to veterinary sites and organizations.

Shows, Expos, and Swap Meets

There are too many herp expos to list them all here, but if you check the show calendar in the latest issue of *Reptiles* magazine, you can find a swap meet or amphibian/reptile show near you. Going to these shows lets you meet breeders and dealers as well as fellow frog and toad enthusiasts. They are a good place to gather information and locate sources of hard-to-find supplies, as well as purchase live animals.

Also search for show venues online. Key words are "reptile shows," "swap-meets," and "expos."

Shopping on the Internet

Here are some mail-order and local pick-up dealers of live frogs and toads, companies that sell live feeder insects, and equipment dealers in the United States, along with their web sites. By including the name of any company in this list, neither the author nor the publisher accepts any responsibility for any commercial dealings between a listed dealer and buyer of frogs, toads, live foods, or supplies. This list is for informational purposes only and no endorsement of any companies or individuals is implied.

Live Frogs and Toads

Arizona Dendrobate Ranch
www.azdr.com

CyberAqua
www.cyberaqua-net.com

Glades Herp Farm
www.gherp.com

Reptile Kingdom
www.reptilekingdom.com

Reptiles-N-Critters
www.reptilesncritters.com/tree_frogs.php

Silver City Serpentarium
www.scserp.com/SCS_Price_List.htm

Xenopus Express
www.xenopus.com

Feeder Insects

Armstrong's Crickets
www.armstrongcrickets.com

BugOrder.Com
www.bugorder.com

Fluker's
www.flukerfarms.com

Ghann's Cricket Farm
www.ghann.com

GrubCo
www.grubco.com

New York Worms
www.nyworms.com

Rainbow Mealworms and Crickets
www.rainbowmealworms.net

Top Hat Cricket Farm
www.tophatcrickets.com

Climate and Humidity Control Equipment

Ecologic Technologies
www.cloudtops.com

Helix Controls
www.helixcontrols.com

Reptronics
www.reptronicsusa.com

Photo Credits
Michael Durand: 41
Isabelle Francais: 8-9, 11, 12, 24, 28, 33, 38, 45, 61, 62, 64, 68-69, 75, 86, 94, 95, 99, 102 (bottom), 104, 107, 108, 110, 116, 117
Bill Love: 1, 4-5, 14, 16, 20, 22, 23, 27, 29, 30, 32, 48, 49, 51, 54, 57, 59, 65, 66, 70, 73, 74, 76, 78, 79, 80, 81, 84, 85, 87, 89, 91, 92, 97, 98, 100, 102 (top), 103, 105, 109, 114, 115
Tammy Rao: 17, 19, 34-35, 36, 37, 39, 40, 44, 50, 53, 55, 58, 72, 120

Index